JOHN PAUL II

A PICTORIAL CELEBRATION

JOHN PAUL II

A PICTORIAL CELEBRATION

Russell Palmer

Our Sunday Visitor, Inc.
Huntington, Indiana 46750

The author and publisher are especially grateful
to those who have graciously allowed the use of
their materials in this work. If any protected materials in this work have been inadvertently used
without permission, we apologize and request
notification from the copyright holder.

Copyright © 1980 by Our Sunday Visitor, Inc.

All rights reserved. No part of this book may be
reproduced or copied in any form or by any
means — graphic, electronic, or mechanical, including photocopying, recording, taping, or information storage and retrieval systems —
without written permission of the publisher.

ISBN: 0-87973-835-9
Library of Congress Catalog Card Number:
79-92691

Published, printed, and bound in the United
States of America

835

Pope John Paul II's official coat of arms symbolizes his special devotion to Mary, the Mother of Christ.

"To every man,
Wherever he may work, believe, suffer,
struggle, sin, love, hate, doubt;
Wherever he may live and die:
I come before him today
with all the truth revealed by the birth
of God and with the message of God."

— JOHN PAUL II

Photo credits

The author wishes to thank the following for the use of their photographs in this book:

Associated Press — pp. 7, 18, 21, 29 (bottom), 32, 37, 39, 45, 52, 53, 58 (bottom left), 59, 61, 73, 79, 83, 91 (top right and bottom), 93, 98, 99, and 112.

Ewing Galloway — p. 25 (top).

Felici — pp. 14, 22, 25 (bottom left), 26 (top), 49, 56, 64-65, 71, 120, and 125.

Mari — pp. 26 (bottom), 42, 58 (top), 60, 63, 67, 72 (top), 94 (top), 95, and 122.

NC News Service — pp. 15, 17, 40, 41, 48, 58 (bottom right), 64, 70, 81, 84-85, 89, 94 (bottom), 101 (bottom left), 102, 105 (bottom), 110, 111 (bottom), 114 (top), 116, 117, 119, and 123.

Our Sunday Visitor, Inc. — pp. 19, 38, 100, 101 (top right), 103, 104, 105 (top), 106, 107, 108, 109, and 111 (top left and right).

Religious News Service — pp. 16, 20, 25 (bottom right), 26, 29 (top), 30, 31, 35, 46, 51, 54, 55, 57, 68, 72 (bottom), 76, 82, 88, 91 (top left), 114 (bottom), 115, and 127.

Author's preface

Millions of words have been written about John Paul II, and more books about him are going to press.

However, if you believe that one picture is worth a thousand words, and that one good picture book is worth a thousand long biographies — this is your book!

Here is your private audience with His Holiness in print . . . your chance to see him in candid close-ups . . . to go with him on emotional pilgrimages . . . to catch his vibes.

The pictures are unretouched news photos. The basic data for the commentary, impressions, and quotes are gathered from a host of periodicals and books we have recommended for further reading in the bibliography at the back.

One cannot study the life of Karol Wojtyla, without learning much about the Mother of God. This book is dedicated to Mary, in gratitude for the gift she has given the world: John Paul II!

—R.P.

Archdiocese of Philadelphia

222 N. 17th Street

Philadelphia, Pa. 19103

Office of the Cardinal

FOREWORD

Seldom has there been such an overwhelming acceptance of, and a response to a newly elected Supreme Pontiff by the peoples of the world, as there has been of Pope John Paul II. When after his election, the Pope greeted and spoke to the crowds in Saint Peter Piazza, the din of the prolonged cheering was deafening. Like others on the balcony, I had to muffle my ears. The thought that the majority of the people in the Piazza were Italian faithful, cheering their PAPA -- their PAPA POLACCO -- was particularly moving. This experience strengthened the appreciation of Our Lord's promise that the Holy Spirit will guide the Church, and that "He will confute the world." He certainly confuted the "experts", the "Vaticanologists", the forecasters.

Because of the increasing numbers requesting admission to the general audiences in the Paul VI Hall, a second audience had to be scheduled in Saint Peter Basilica, and then a third one in the Audience Hall. Finally, the general audiences were moved to the Piazza. In the course of a normal week, at least 70,000, and at times over 100,000 people gather in the Piazza on Wednesday and Sunday to see and hear Pope John Paul II.

The Pope's magnetic attraction was evident to the world when millions of people came to see and hear him on his pilgrimage of faith to the churches in the Dominican Republic, Mexico, and Poland. When I returned from the Holy Father's Pilgrimage to Poland, peoples of various religious and non-religious convictions were anxious to hear and to learn more about Pope John Paul II.

People are generally fascinated by the person and the message of the Holy Father. They desire to know more about his magnetism, his charism. It is easy to say that Pope John Paul was born in a small Polish village, one of two sons of a plebian family; that he was a rugged man of the people, who worked in a quarry and a chemical factory; that before he reached the age of 21, both his parents and his only sibling had died; that he had to go under cover and was wanted for helping Jews, and other fugitives from the Nazi persecution; that he was involved in dealing with a government hostile to religion.

It is easy to say that before his election he traveled throughout the world, preaching at various functions - including at the Philadelphia International Eucharistic Congress, and lecturing at various institutions - including the Harvard and Catholic Universities in the United States.   It is easy to say that the list of his published writings - including books - included more than 190;   that he was a poet, a playwright, and author, a professor, a lecturer, a renowned philosopher and theologian, a retreat master who gave a spiritual retreat to his predecessor Paul VI, a linguist, a prelate who played an important role in the II Vatican Council, the Synod of Bishops, and a member of Sacred Congregations in Rome.

Like each of us, John Paul II is a unique individual.   He eludes the facile labeling of liberal/conservative.   He is a very public person, perfectly at ease with all levels of peoples.   Yet he is a very private person, at peace with himself - totally unassuming, deeply spiritual almost to the point of mysticism.   He is anxious to conform to God's will and the promptings of the Holy Spirit, totally dedicated to truth and courageous in proclaiming it.

Russell Palmer, who provided us with a candid portrait and practically a private audience with Pope Paul VI in his book: "You Could Not Come to Me..So I have Come To You", is using his expertise to provide us with a candid insight into Pope John Paul II.

My best recommendation of this volume cannot possibly match the merits of its contents.   The readers will certainly be enriched, and will gain an intimate appreciation of the warm, spiritual man whom we call, Our Holy Father.

JOHN CARDINAL KROL
Archbishop of Philadelphia

July 9, 1979

INSIDE . . .

Prologue: Seventy-eight days that shook the Catholic world

L'OSSERVATORE ROMANO

VATICAN CITY
EDITORIAL AND MANAGEMENT OFFICES

WEEKLY EDITION ✠ IN ENGLISH

UNICUIQUE SUUM   NON PRAEVALEBUNT

ELEVENTH YEAR

Price: 200 lire

N. 41 (550) · October 12, 1978

Annual Subscription: ORDINARY MAIL: $17.00 U.S. (£10.00); AIR MAIL: Europe $24.00 U.S. (£13.00); North America $28.00 U.S.; Central and South America $23.00 U.S.; Africa $23.00 U.S.; Asia $26.00 U.S.; Oceania (Australia and New Zealand) $30.00 U.S. · Subscriptions payable to the Management Office, L'Osservatore Romano, Vatican City · Advertising Agency A. MANZONI and Co., Milan, V. Agnello 12, tel. 272.186; Rome, Via del Corso 207, tel. 679.4091 · Vatican City, Via del Pellegrino · Advertising Rates (col. mm.) Commercial 400 lire; Obituary 500 lire; Personel Notices 600 lire; Financial 700 lire

CARDINAL CONFALONIERI DELIVERS HOMILY

Funeral Mass for Pope John Paul I

During the celebration of the funeral rite for Pope John Paul I, which took place in St Peter's Square at four p.m. on Wednesday, 4 October, the Dean of the Sacred College, Cardinal Carlo Confalonieri delivered the following homily.

Venerable Brothers in Jesus Christ,

No one would have thought that less than two months after we celebrated the funeral rites in St Peter's Square of Pope Paul VI, who died suddenly, we would once again be gathered here to say our final farewell to his successor, our Holy Father John Paul I. He died so suddenly after only 33 days of his pontificate.

We ask ourselves, why so quickly? The Apostle tells us why in the well-known and beloved explanation: "How deep his wisdom and knowledge and how impossible to penetrate his motives or understand his methods!... Who could ever know the mind of the Lord?" (Rom 11:33). Thus is presented to us, in all its immense and almost oppressive greatness, the unfathomable mystery of life and of death. We have scarcely had the time to see the new Pope. Yet one month was enough for him to have conquered hearts—and, for us, it was a month to love him intensely. It is not length which characterizes a life in a pontificate, but rather the spirit that fills it. He passed as a meteor which unexpectedly lights up the heavens and then disappears, leaving us amazed and astonished. Already the Book of Wisdom (4:13) spoke of this when telling of "the just man": "Coming to perfection in such short time he achieved long life." "Consumatus in brevi, explevit tempora multa". The funeral prayer which we are soon to recite brings this comforting touch of reality: "Grant O Lord that he may praise you without end in heaven, he who on earth served you with a constant profession of faith."

Instinctive goodness

In Pope John Paul we greeted and venerated the Vicar of Christ, Bishop of Rome and Supreme Pastor of the universal Church; but in the brief contact had with him, we were quickly struck and fascinated by his instinctive goodness, by his innate modesty, by his sincere simplicity in deed and word. The very papal allocutions themselves—the few that he was able to give—reflect this quality. It began with the first discourse that he gave in the Sistine Chapel on the day after his election (for him, how unexpected and how

Continued on Page 2, Col. 1 ●

Threatening rain with occasional downpours did not deter the thousands of persons from participating in the funeral service for Pope John Paul I, which was held out of doors on Wednesday afternoon, 4 October.

The startling string of events in Rome in the fall of 1978 was a news happening that caught the attention of the entire world. This was an epic time. To bring it to you, this section condenses the actual news stories of the time, with only a few paragraphs of added commentary. Most of the credit goes to the news services who reported history in the making.

On August 6, 1978, Pope Paul VI asked those around him to "pray for me." A short time later, at 9:40 p.m., he was dead. He died so peacefully that his aides at first thought he had only fallen asleep. So ended the remarkable fifteen-year pontificate of a beloved pastor who exhausted himself coping with the problems of the post-Vatican Church.

Who could succeed one of the most experienced and capable popes in history? As the world awaited the results of what was expected to be a lengthy debate, the answer came with stunning swiftness. The largest gathering of cardinals in conclave history reached agreement on August 26. A "dark horse," the humble patriarch of Venice, Albino Luciani, was raised to the highest post in Christendom. And, for Romans, it was literally a case of love at first sight. There were few dry eyes as the throng greeted the smiling "servant of the servants of God."

Then, a little over a month later, John Paul I was dead. Once again, all eyes were on Rome. Once again, the cardinals flew to Rome to elect a new pope — this time shattering tradition by choosing, on October 16, the first non-Italian in four hundred fifty-five years: Cardinal Karol Wojtyla of Krakow, Poland. There were other surprises as well: that the new pope was so young, only fifty-eight, at the time of his election; that he comes from the East; and that he is the first Polish pope in the Church's history.

Rarely has such a series of dramatic and historic events unfolded under the glare of unprecedented news coverage. Around the world a television audience estimated at one billion watched the vigorous new pope from the East, John Paul II, receive the pallium of authority as the Supreme Pastor of the world's more than seven hundred million Catholics. The emotional scene ended a brief span of seventy-eight days that rank among the most dramatic times in the two-thousand-year history of the Roman Church. Wojtyla chose the name of John in tribute to Pope John XXIII who called Vatican Council II . . . Paul, in tribute to his own mentor, Paul VI . . . and John Paul in tribute to his predecessor, John Paul I, who established himself as "the pope of goodness" in a few days.

I close my eyes on this sad, dramatic, and magnificent world, calling God's charity down on it once more.
— Pope Paul VI (1963-1978)

The September Pope: John Paul I (August 26- September 28, 1978)

At 7:17 p.m., on August 26, nearly an hour after the first puffs of grayish-white smoke had appeared, Cardinal Pericle Felici stood on the balcony of St. Peter's and ended the suspense for the huge crowd below. *"Annuntio vobis gaudium magnum,"* he said. *"Habemus papam."* ("I announce to you a great joy. We have a pope.") He continued, "He is . . . His Most Eminent and Reverend Lordship, Lord Albino Cardinal Luciani . . . who has taken for himself the name John Paul I. . . .

At the announcement of the new pope's chosen name, John Paul I, the crowd broke into wild applause.

Banners, signs, and handkerchiefs were waved in the air as more than one hundred thousand people waited in the square for the first appearance and apostolic blessing from the former patriarch of Venice who had just become the 262nd bishop of Rome and head of the world's Catholics.

The choice of the engagingly humble Cardinal Luciani, a dark horse and the third pope in the twentieth century to come from Venice, was immediately interpreted as showing a clear desire by the cardinals to have a pastoral pope.

The new pope's choice of the double name, John Paul, was immediately understood as a sign he intended to continue the policies and style of his predecessor. At 7:32, an adoring crowd roared its approval as John Paul I appeared for the first time in public and opened his arms to the people below.

He smiled broadly — with the smile that would become the hallmark of his short papacy.

It was the cardinals who elected the new pope; it was the people who embraced him. Once more, the square was alive with waving banners, scarves, handkerchiefs, and cries of *"Viva il Papa!"* All Rome roared its welcome.

On September 29, Pope John Paul I, whose surprise election only the previous month had catapulted him into the world's limelight, died quietly and alone in the Apostolic Palace on the thirty-fourth day of his pontificate. Death came at 11:00 p.m., September 28, from a heart attack. Only hours earlier, in his last public address, the pope spoke of Christ's promise of eternal life.

John Paul I was like "a meteor that lights up the heavens and then disappears, leaving us amazed and astonished." So spoke Cardinal Carlo Confalonieri, dean of the Sacred College of Cardinals. Millions of the world's people agreed. The promise, the sincerity, along with the humanity and warmth of "the pope of goodness and the smile," was obvious in his every gesture.

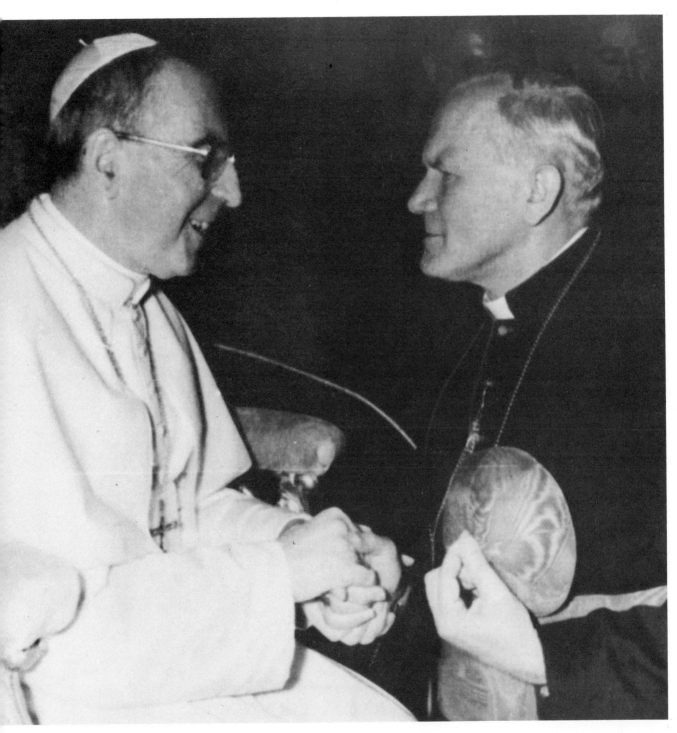

The late John Paul I greets Polish Cardinal Karol Wojtyla during the first audience after his election.

How popes are elected

Ever since the Third Lateran Council of 1179, selection of the new pope has been the work of the College of Cardinals, meeting in Rome.

Voting itself is done in the awesome Sistine Chapel where the cardinals meet and pray for divine guidance. When the early ballots are counted and no one man has been elected, they are burned with damp straw. This causes black smoke to rise from the small chimney installed for the election. When a pope is finally chosen (by two thirds of the vote, plus one) the ballots are burned without straw and the white smoke heralds the news to the world.

Two votes are taken each morning, two in the afternoon, with the cardinals voting in order of seniority. Each one must pray, "I take witness to Christ Our Lord, who is to judge me, that I have voted for him who, before God, I feel should be elected."

The Holy Spirit is an acknowledged factor in papal elections. One story goes that a pope, St. Fabian (236-250 A.D.), was actually elected when a dove flew down and settled on his head in a remarkable imitation of the descent of the Holy Spirit in the form of a dove on the Savior.

One thing is certain. The speculations of men matter little in a papal election. When Paul VI died, there was intense debate about a dozen leading candidates, who seemed to tower above all others. Yet the final selection, made swiftly and reflecting unbounded enthusiasm, was a complete surprise to the "experts." Even Cardinal Luciani himself had scoffed at reporters who suggested he might become a pope.

Upon John Paul's death, even greater speculation excited a world now turning its full attention to Vatican affairs. Once again, the result was a stunning surprise. And, once again, the assembled cardinals expressed their joy at the ease with which they had come to an agreement on their choice, the first Polish pope, Karol Wojtyla.

**John Paul II:
A pope
to change the world!**

On October 16, as a crowd estimated at three hundred thousand roared its approval, a new era was announced for the Roman Catholic Church. Shortly after six on the evening of the second day of balloting to elect a successor to John Paul I, white smoke appeared in a steady stream from the chimney on the roof of the Sistine Chapel. Moments later, a window opened on a balcony above the entrance to St. Peter's, and Cardinal Felici held up his arms to the crowd, requesting silence.

Just six weeks previously, the cardinal had appeared on that same balcony, beaming at the crowd below to announce the election of Cardinal Albino Luciani as Supreme Pastor of the Church. Now, Cardinal Felici seemed more subdued, and he seemed to hesitate over the foreign name as he announced to the Roman crowd that the choice of the conclave was the cardinal-archbishop of Krakow, Karol Wojtyla.

Karol Wojtyla. The first pope from Eastern Europe. The first from Poland, a nation whose fervor for Catholicism has been unsurpassed for a millennium. The first pope, in a real sense, to prove by his nationality the universality of the modern Church.

Joyfully, the throng quickly accepted the idea of a non-Italian bishop of Rome. "The pope is for the world," said one elderly Italian woman. "We're all one Church," said a nun. Indeed, the initial words of John Paul II to the people were in a surprisingly well-accented Italian: *"Sia lodato Gesu Cristo!"* ("May Jesus Christ be praised!")

"Dearest brothers and sisters," he continued, "we are still saddened over the death of our most beloved Pope John Paul I. And now the most eminent cardinals have called a new bishop to Rome. They have called him from a faraway nation . . . distant . . . but ever close in the communion of faith and Christian tradition.

"With fear I received this nomination," he went on. "But I have accepted it in obedience to Our Lord and to the Mother of God.

"I speak to you in our Italian language [applause], so correct me if I make mistakes." (Wild applause!)

He ended by saying, "And so I present myself to you all to confess our common faith, our hope, and our confidence in the Mother of the Church and also to set forth on this road of the Church with the aid of God and with the aid of men."

Immediately, the hundreds of thousands in the square broke into explosive applause and waved banners upward toward the floodlit central balcony of the world's most famous church. Most happy of all were a large number of Polish pilgrims who had just arrived in Rome, surprised and delighted to be witnesses to their cardinal's election.

In later interviews, the theologians of the Church were as thrilled as the laity with the election of John Paul II. Those who had participated with him in international theological meetings testified to the depth of his philosophical intelligence and ability to relate traditional Catholic thought to contemporary intellectual movements.

The new pope not only took an active part in the deliberations of the Vatican Council, but he has also participated in every one of the synods of bishops held in Rome since the Council. In 1976, Pope Paul VI invited him to preach the Lenten retreat for the Roman Curia.

History will judge his reign. But in his first year he has already established himself as a warm and loving pastor, a surprisingly energetic evangelizer, a defender of human rights, and a charismatic figure who is already acknowledged as a world leader. He is a master of diplomacy and of the media. And he knows how to present a strong message of fidelity to the crucified and risen Christ in a way that wins the hearts and souls of his audience.

Another hallmark of his papacy is his devotion to Mary, as well as a deep prayer life that takes precedence no matter how busy he is on his many pilgrimages.

In everything he does, this new pope has a way of breaking tradition, winning hearts. When he spoke to the Sacred College of Cardinals for the first time as pope, instead of giving the traditional blessing, he asked them to bless one another. He could have hardly found a better way to inspire their loyalty and support than to treat them as equals.

His entire career has been characterized by outstanding zeal for the word of God, total generosity in the service of the poor and heroic commitment to the cause of human rights.

— *Bishop Thomas Kelly, O.P.*

One newspaper in Lima, Peru, greeted Wojtyla's election with the headline: LABORER, POET, ACTOR, PRIEST, POPE! Wojtyla is all that and more: quarryman and factory worker, active member of Poland's underground, professor of philosophy and ethics, pastor with a common touch. On top of that he is an outdoorsman who loved to ski on Poland's Tatra Mountains, to kayak or canoe on the Mazurian Lakes, to climb mountains and hike. To play the guitar.

This new pope, only fifty-eight when he began his reign, "works like an ox, sleeps very little, and is very open, especially to youth," said Polish Bishop Boleslaw Babrowski in a radio interview. He added that he is also "very devoted to the Blessed Mother, and prays the Way of the Cross every day."

John Paul II tells the cardinals: "It was an act of trust and an act of courage to call a 'non-Italian' to be the Bishop of Rome."

21

Yes, if there is a place where all people should come together in peace and mutual respect, with sensitivity, with a sincere desire for their dignity, their goodness, their progress, it is certainly at the heart of the Church, near the Holy See, established to give witness to the truth and love of Christ.
— *John Paul II*

Welcome to the . . . VATICAN STATE and your audience

The Vatican is a mini-state with an area of only one hundred seven acres. But it has its own railway station on a siding which links it with the main rail network of Italy. There is even a real iron curtain that can be dropped to shut off the siding. The Vatican City's newspaper is *L'Osservatore Romano,* published in many languages, with a circulation of ninety thousand.

The Vatican State has two hundred fifty registered autos, a fire department, a police force, and an army. Its national anthem was written by Gounod, while Marconi designed its radio tower. It is said that the radio pioneer got his inspiration for radio while he was walking in a cathedral. He dedicated his first broadcast to Mary, the Mother of God. Today, the Vatican Radio broadcasts to the world in thirty-three languages.

The palace gardens, which are the only open ground in this tiny state, are well planned. Flowers bloom all the year round, and blossoming shrubs and exotic plants give variety to the scene, enhanced by splashing fountains and little shrines hidden away in unexpected corners.

Everyone knows about the Swiss Guards with their resplendent costumes designed by Michelangelo. But the Vatican also has other armed bodies — the Noble Guard, chosen from among the aristocracy to act as honorary escort for the pope; the Palatine Guard, the main body of Vatican forces, and the Papal Gendarmes, the regular police force in Napoleonic uniforms.

There are also the Privy Chamberlains of Cape and Sword, dressed in Spanish costume.

The Swiss Guards are real soldiers. History records their heroic defense of Pope Clement VII against the more powerful forces of Charles of Bourbon in 1527. Nearly one hundred fifty Swiss Guards were slaughtered in the Piazza di San Pietro, on the steps of the basilica, and near the main altar. May 6, the anniversary of the decimation of the guards, is set aside each year for a colorful service of commemoration and for the swearing in of new guards to protect the Holy Father.

The present Vatican is a rather haphazard collection of buildings because of additions made through the centuries, but the main part of it was built in the fourteenth and fifteenth centuries. The palace contains over ten thousand rooms and halls and nine hundred ninety-seven stairways, thirty of which are secret.

The Vatican City telephone directory has over one hundred fifty pages of listings, including such oddities as a number for the monument to Pope Pius X. One number you will not find, however, is the private line of John Paul II. The papal number is known only to those who must have it. And even they still have to get past the pope's vigilant staff.

Dozens of calls for the pope are placed daily by the troubled or curious from all over the world. A nun of the Pious Disciples of the Divine Master, the religious order which provides the Vatican telephone operators, will pass such calls on to an appropriate official of the Vatican Secretariat of State. The Vatican directory contains several surprises, such as a number for calling the funeral monument of Pope Benedict XIV and another for the monument of Pope St. Pius X, among the eighteen lines installed in St. Peter's Basilica. The reason is that inside these large monuments two first-aid stations have been installed to meet emergency needs during crowded papal audiences.

Vatican finances are no longer a closely guarded secret since John Paul II has recently called for a full disclosure. One point worth making is that the great art treasures of the Vatican State, often cited as part of its wealth, are actually a trust, and cost a great deal to protect against decay and thievery.

The Vatican's greatest resource is its permanence. Art may fade, economies grow and decline, but the Vatican itself endures through one changing world after another.

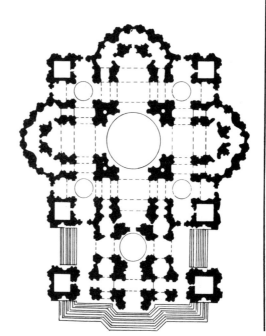

Right (clockwise): Aerial view of the Vatican State. Jubilant crowds. Swearing in of Swiss Guards.

Left: Basic floor plan of St. Peter's Basilica.

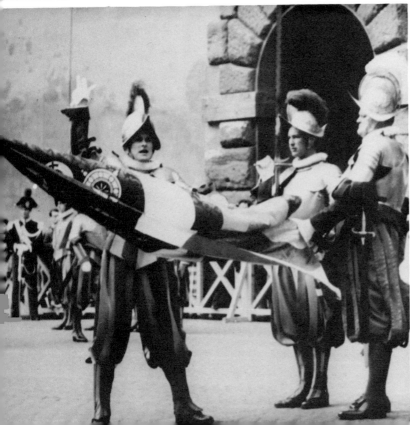

John Paul II seldom resists the chance to have a personal encounter with his audience, to the delight of the crowd.

PREFETTURA DELLA CASA PONTIFICIA

Permesso personale per partecipare all'Udienza del Santo Padre che avrà luogo in Piazza San Pietro, mercoledì 27 giugno 1979, alle ore 18.

REPARTO S. PAOLO
Ingresso: Colonnato di destra
(davanti al Portone di Bronzo)

№ 1064

Il biglietto è del tutto gratuito.

Viva il Papa!

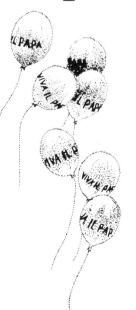

Catholic, Protestant, Jew; pilgrim, politician, businessman, refugee, or sophisticated world traveler: all share one desire in common — a longing to see the pope in person.

Now that supersonic jets have eased the burden of travel and a charismatic and crowd-pleasing pope awaits them in Rome, the crowds of tourists and pilgrims have reached ungovernable proportions.

The papal audiences have already been moved outdoors to St. Peter's Square from the huge new Paul VI Audience Hall so that crowds as large as one hundred thousand can satisfy their craving to see this Polish pope. He brings a unique wave of excitement to the audiences these days that tops the most dramatic moments of the recent Holy Year. Each Wednesday, the huge square is thronged with people dashing madly to find a vantage point with only a slim chance of a personal encounter — even as one person in a crowd of a hundred thousand — with the popular pope who loves crowds, and children, and youth.

John Paul is undoubtedly the most exciting public figure in the world today. And he is especially dear to the Italians. The mayor of Rome has had to ask that the papal audiences be delayed from 11:00 a.m. to 6:00 p.m. to alleviate the five-hour traffic jams caused by cars rushing toward the Vatican.

When the square does fill and the pope finally arrives, a solid phalanx of bodies presses forward. Arms wave.

Applause breaks out like sudden rain. There are shouts of *"Santita! Santita!"* ("Holiness! Holiness!")

Above the heads you see a man in white riding in a white jeep. It is Pope John Paul II. He leans down with arms outstretched to brush the grasping forest of fingers reaching up from the crowd. Infants are held aloft for blessing. A woman faints and is carried to a first-aid station.

> **"He has known poverty and the difficult times of war. He understands us. He is one of us."**

The sheer size of the crowd has made the weekly general audience a Roman spectacle. But it is not to be put down. Its very overcrowding, its emotions, make it a microcosm of the world today with all its faults and virtues. To be there, to see a mother with tears holding up a sick baby for a papal blessing, to see nuns silently praying a Rosary in the midst of mass confusion, to see a tired band of villagers who had walked miles on foot to attend, to hear a group of Polish pilgrims singing a mountain song they know John Paul would wish to hear — all of this defies description.

What strikes the observer about John Paul II is his genuine vitality. He seems very healthy in mind and body. A natural man, without pretense, he looks directly at each individual he greets personally, totally unaware of cameras and TV. His open, honest, smiling face is enriched by a lively, concerned expression. Frequently, those who have received a greeting or blessing from him report that they'll "never be the same again!"

His asides, when he puts away his prepared texts, are looked forward to and treasured by everyone. After one audience, an Austrian woman summed up his appeal, "He has known poverty and the difficult times of war. He understands us. He is one of us."

No wonder that the audiences are now one of Rome's prime attractions. How do you get in on them?

There is no special procedure. Tickets are free, on a first-come, first-served basis. Most Americans place their requests through the Office for Papal Audiences of the North American College, Via dell' Umilta, 30, 00187, Rome. The Jesuit Guest Bureau at Borgo Santo Spirito, as well as the Paulist Fathers at the American National Church of Santa Susanna, takes care of many requests.

You can also write directly to the Prefect of the Apostolic Palace, Vatican City. The letter can be in English, should specify the date you wish to attend, and where the ticket can be delivered to you in Rome. Your note should also be accompanied by a letter of introduction from a priest or someone responsible writing on a letterhead. This letter of introduction can be from a non-Catholic. The purpose is to screen out cranks.

American visitors can get passes for general audiences by applying to the Bishops' Office for United States Visitors to the Vatican, Casa Santa Maria, Via dell' Umilta, 30, 00187, Rome.

If you are in Rome and haven't made arrangements to attend an audience, your best bet is to call the American parish church of Santa Susanna.

Santa Susanna submits its requests to the Vatican just twenty-four hours before an audience and will even deliver the tickets to your hotel!

Groups of ten or more, though, should always write ahead. For U.S. servicemen and their dependents there

Kissing a baby at the St. Antonio de Padua Church in downtown Rome . . . and holding a wooden cross given to him by pilgrims at the Sanctuary of Divine Love nine miles south of Rome.

Papal audiences are now the number one tourist attraction in Rome.

is a third alternative: the USO club near the Vatican on Via Della Conciliazione 2, which gets about four hundred tickets a week.

Ticket holders should remember that seats are not numbered, except for the special front-row seats which give you a good chance to exchange a word with the pontiff. Instead, they are simply marked in sections A to D, with A being closest to the pope. Plan to be there early if you want to be near the front or at a vantage point on an aisle.

Should you try to take in an audience at the very last moment, try the North American College. Two hours before the audience starts, all uncollected tickets are put up for grabs. So much for security!

Failing that, go to St. Peter's Square and stand at the back. You'll see the pope as he circles in his white jeep, and you'll also have easy access to the ice-cream vendor at the back of the huge, horseshoe-shaped piazza, a welcome advantage under the Mediterranean sun.

In any case, there are no longer private audiences other than those granted a few public figures. The general audience is your only chance to see John Paul II.

As a footnote, at one general audience when crowds were smaller, and the audiences more intimate, a visitor actually slipped the Fisherman's Ring from the hand of Pius XII — unnoticed — and started toward the door. Luckily, an alert and aghast chamberlain finally caught sight of the precious ring and it was returned.

Paul VI, in a historic, ecumenical gesture, took off his ring and gave it to the archbishop of Canterbury, spiritual leader of the Anglican Church. The pope said it was "not yet the ring of matrimony, but a ring of engagement."

On another occasion, a venerable old man approached Paul VI after a ceremony in St. Peter's. His message was *"Coraggio, Santo Padre, coraggio!"* ("Courage, Holy Father, courage!") He was Saverio Roncalli, John XXIII's brother. Paul VI said later he felt as though he was listening to a message from his predecessor.

A band of jubilant
gypsies greets the
pontiff.

Street scene in Mexic

A new papal life-style

Vatican insiders have it that during an early public appearance by John Paul II, when he went overtime talking to special groups, an attendant whispered persistently, *"Basta!"* ("Enough!") The pope turned quickly to the aide at his shoulder and said, "Shh! I am the pope, and I know what I am doing!"

Agreed! In a world looking desperately for leadership, we have at last a man of faith, who knows where he is going, what he is doing, and why. No wonder that the world press seems agreed that he is the only man of stature on the international scene today.

A sign of this is his appearance on the cover of *Newsweek* five times in one year and on *Time's* cover four times.

A longtime press aide to His Holiness, John Szostak, writes, "He is in tune with the times."

Protestant theologian George Williams says of him, "In a most remarkable way, he is a man whose soul is at leisure with himself." Wojtyla is his own man, a man who eludes the usual labels of conservative or liberal. He sings, cuts red tape, says what he thinks.

The result? He is electrifying. John Paul is drawing record crowds to Rome. On his pilgrimages he has been greeted by millions, with banners, applause, shouts, and song. The roar of the crowds, according to some princes of the Church, is often so loud they have to muffle their ears. Huge crowds press forward to touch the pontiff, or his vestments, to feel blessed by the contact. He advances unhurriedly through each adoring throng, radiating vitality and a magnetic, irresistible current of warmth and contagious good humor.

John Paul is at home with everyone. Early in his reign, he told one Roman crowd, "Our meeting has been very warm, very noisy, and I hope very religious." To his credit, priests report he is attracting five times the number of penitents to the confessional than ever before.

He is the star of a new disco album, and the idol of press, radio, and TV where "he fills the whole screen." Says Cesare Pagini, bishop of Citta di Castello: "The arrival of Pope John Paul has turned our youth upside down. They are seeking leadership once again, to advance not only the ecclesiastical but the civil life of our country." On all the pope's many pilgrimages, he gets his most enthusiastic welcome from young people who have almost made him into a cult figure.

> **"In a most remarkable way, he is a man whose soul is at leisure with himself."**

John Paul seems tireless. Journalists report they do not cover him, they pursue him! Even after a difficult audience is over, after he has talked for over an hour in a half-dozen languages, he tarries behind, conversing expansively with groups from many countries. In the rear, the neglected ones try to coax him into song by singing a favorite hymn or mountain song. To their delight, they sometimes succeed!

If there is a common denominator in all Wojtyla's appearances and utterances it is his obsession with man, *man on earth.* Like John XXIII, he tells us: *"Man first, then the rest."*

As a pastor, John Paul has already begun the most forceful campaign in favor of political, economic, and social rights in the history of the modern Church since Leo XIII issued his landmark encyclical, *Rerum Novarum,* in 1891.

People everywhere sense this love of mankind instantly, and respond to it, as they did to Pope John XXIII. And that encouraging response helps His Holiness get through a long day. He is up at 5:00 a.m., praying, writing, and receiving private visitors, while busy assistants constantly remind him of the full schedule planned for the afternoon and evening. He then eats a hearty breakfast of fried ham and sausage, and reads *L'Unita,* the Italian Communist daily, from front to back to keep up with his critics.

> **"He is a perfect triangle — a man of God, a man of intellect, and a man of great heart."**

At 8:30 he goes down one floor to the official papal library where he begins the day's work. He tries to get his own workload out of the way before he begins a long schedule of meetings.

At lunch, he meets with the local priests of his diocese, Rome, with Vatican officials and friends, and with occasional visitors from other countries. The pope himself often mixes the salad and heaps the plates of his guests with a liberal dosing of ground Parmesan. After a fifteen-minute rest — instead of the traditional hour's siesta — he walks two miles at a brisk pace with his Polish secretary, Don Stanislau Dziwioz, also an athlete and skier.

What keeps this Renaissance man going?

Perhaps it is his absolute enjoyment at serving as the spiritual leader of the world's seven hundred million Roman Catholics. He acts as though he has finally come into his own in this most difficult office. For him it is not the killing burden that it was for Albino Luciani, his predecessor.

John Paul's Polish friends are convinced he deeply believes that his God-given mission is to lead his badly troubled Church into the third millennium of Christendom as a revivified institution, fully in tune with the modern world.

Whatever he plans for the future, at this moment he is a man willing to change and to grow. He has often expressed his warm desire to work well with his fellow bishops. To this end he has called all the world's cardinals to Rome, to begin an unprecedented dialogue that should help the Church keep pace with the needs of the modern world. Of course, like most good politicians, John Paul tends to move cautiously, profiting from the best thinking of his contemporaries.

His unrestrained goodwill has already won assurances from the tough Polish leader, Henryk Jablonski, that his homeland's doors will always be open to him.

All in all, there hasn't been anyone like this tough, realistic pope in the long history of the Vatican. The first pope from Eastern Europe. The first from Poland. The first non-Italian elected since 1523. The youngest pope since 1846. And, clearly, one of the most vigorous and strong-minded of pontiffs. Vatican bureaucrats no longer speculate: Who has his ear? He is obviously his own man.

No wonder that all Rome is bewildered by his actions, his innovations, and his disregard for protocol.

Above: The pope asks the crowd for permission to leave.

Below: Like a good sport, John Paul makes the most of a gift balloon.

John Paul's informality is now his trademark. During the Mexican trip, he happily donned sombreros. In Poland, he stopped in the middle of discourses to start humming a folk song. In New York's Harlem, he joined blacks in a Negro spiritual. Back in Rome, he still breaks precedent daily.

On the literary side, his output is prodigious. Every day he spends time composing, while walking through the relaxing Vatican gardens. Then he returns to his study to pen homilies, messages, greetings, and scores of personal letters. He has written ten books.

There's so much more to Wojtyla that it would take volumes to get him down on paper, to encompass all his interests. He is, after all, a scholar and mystic, a theologian, linguist, actor and playwright, poet, a worker and a daring skier, hiker, and canoeist, a guitarist and singer, an intellectual and an outdoorsman, and a patriot who served courageously in the underground.

In one recent poll, he was voted the "outstanding personality" of the '70s.

His meeting with the patriarch of the Orthodox Church, Dimitrios I of Constantinople, has already been hailed as the major ecumenical event of the last year and probably of the whole decade. If it leads to actual reunion, it will draw together the two largest Christian bodies — nearly seven hundred twenty-five million Roman Catholics and more than two hundred million Orthodox — into a single church.

His secret?

One old Polish priest summed it all up well. "He is a perfect triangle — a man of God, a man of intellect, and a man of great heart."

One sure key to his personality is his eternal restlessness. In his first talk with John Paul after his election, Cardinal Franz Koenig of Austria asked the new holy Father, "So — how's the pope?" The reply: "Champing at the bit to get outside."

That "champing at the bit" can explain this exuberant pontiff's frequent trips to Castel Gandolfo, his new swimming pool, his tours of working-class districts, his two hours of exercise every day, his pilgrimages to Mexico, Poland, Ireland, the United States, Turkey, his impromptu visits to Curia offices in the Vatican, and his desire for involvement in world affairs.

John Paul II is one Christian leader who may, through truly passionate Christian zeal, actually change our world. He is "a man formed by the Council," inspired by it, impatient to see all its fruits in our lives. He is not a man to be taken lightly.

In 1848, Julius Slowacki, a beloved Polish poet and dramatist, wrote these prophetic words:

We need strength to lift
this world of God;
Thus here comes a Slavic Pope,
a brother of the people,
And he already pours the
balms of the world
on our bosoms,
And the angels' chorus
sweeps his throne with
flowers.

Typical scenes (clockwise): Passing a child back to his parents; receiving a gift of skis; leaving Rome in a helicopter to avoid causing a traffic jam.

John Paul loves children — and their response is sometimes overwhelming!

Christ loves childhood, which is the mistress of humility, the measure of innocence, the example of sweetness.

— *St. Leo*

As you return home to your children, hug them and say: This is the embrace of the pope.

— *John XXIII*

Dear Pope John Paul II,
I would like to take part in helping the poor, by giving up deserts, to people who aren't as well off as my family and I. I will try to donate as much money to the poor, as I can.

Love,
Karyn Kwiatkowski

P.S.
{ I am polish too! }

Thirty-six-foot-long letter to the pope: Students at St. Mary's School, Littleton, Colorado, work on a collective letter to Pope John Paul II. (Karyn Kwiatkowski wrote her own personal note.)

Among his many titles, Christ is called a little child. To illustrate . . . you have struck a child, you have hurt him . . . but you show him a kindness . . . you give him a flower, a rose, or some other object he likes. Instantly, he runs to embrace you. Thus it is with Christ. You offer Him the flower of contrition . . . at once He forgets your offense, He forgives you your sin, He runs, He takes you in His arms, and gives you the kiss of peace.

— *St. Anthony of Padua*

What does a pope do?

> *You are 'Rock', and on this rock I will build my church, and the jaws of death shall not prevail against it. I will entrust to you the keys of the kingdom of heaven."*
>
> **MATTHEW 16:18**

John Paul II is still a priest . . . a shepherd . . . a humble servant of the servants of God.

"The service of Peter," he says, "is essentially a commitment of dedication and love. My humble ministry seeks to be just that."

What does a pope do? What is his role in the world?

Pope Paul warned us that "the papacy is a mystery."

In the final sense, that is true. Yet the casual observer of the modern papacy is impressed more by the long list of day-to-day functions today's pope is heir to. In a world desperate for leaders he stands virtually alone on the world stage. His voice carries more and more authority as the voice of Christians everywhere. Billy Graham says, "When the pope speaks, the world listens."

John Paul II is the spiritual shepherd of more than seven hundred million Roman Catholics scattered throughout the world. He is also the head of Vatican City, a demanding job, overseeing an extensive network of nine congregations, three tribunals, three secretariats, a complex of twenty-six commissions and councils, and additional offices and bureaus headed by the Vatican Secretariat of State and the Council for the Public Affairs of the Church.

For three hundred sixty-five days a year he has to be available . . . to each and every individual.

The Holy Father is also the bishop of Rome itself. And he takes that duty seriously. He has started to make good his promise to visit every parish church in Rome, a city crowded with churches. Parish priests in the Eternal City are ecstatic when the pope invites them to dinner and discusses the problems of their individual parishes.

He leads the people of Rome, over the Vatican Radio, in a weekly recitation of the Rosary. He has told the Communist mayor of Rome that he "feels co-responsible" for the people of Rome and their welfare. Coming from Wojtyla, this is an implied warning that the mayor had better put the welfare of the Roman citizenry above all else, or he will hear from the Vatican.

John Paul is also the primate of Italy. He spends much additional time looking after the spiritual health of the nation. He has asked doctors to resist public pressure for abortions. He has appealed to kidnappers to release hostages. He has had many busy meetings with the president of Italy.

On the international scene, he sent Cardinal Antonio Samore, the "Vatican Kissinger," on a mission of shuttle diplomacy credited with averting a possible war between Chile and Argentina. He intends to visit these countries personally when all the wounds are healed.

On national TV, a Protestant leader has suggested that the world should turn to John Paul II to find a solution to the conflict between Israel and the Palestinians.

The pope is a dedicated pilgrim of peace, as the pages of this book show the reader. He has already been to Mexico, Poland, Ireland, Turkey, and the U.S., where he spoke before the United Nations. At this writing he plans innumerable other trips.

Within his first year of office he issued a clear call for evangelization, international church cooperation, and reminded Europeans of their Christian roots.

In one week, early in his reign, this tireless pope held a private audience with the president of France, resumed an extensive review of Vatican personnel, held a doubleheader general audience, and talked for twenty minutes in German to visitors from West Germany, Austria, Holland, and Switzerland. Then he spoke in Italian, French, English, and Spanish to a second group, lecturing them smilingly on the virtues of prudence.

He went to Castel Gandolfo, outside Rome, where a delirious crowd of townspeople swarmed around him. He kissed their babies, shook their hands, addressed them from the papal balcony, sang a few verses of a Polish song for them, and then carefully surveyed the grounds of the papal estate.

As one papal bodyguard put it, mopping his brow during a moment's respite, "I don't know what it's doing to His Holiness, but the pace is killing me."

In his first year, John Paul II issued a far-ranging document on the nature and goals of catechetics and also found time to issue his first encyclical, *Redemptor Hominis,* which has already been hailed by scholars and theologians as a landmark document in the long history of the Church. Its first words are a ringing rejection of the opening of the *Communist Manifesto.* Marx wrote: "The history of all hitherto existing society has been the history of class struggles." John Paul writes: "The redeemer of man, Jesus Christ, is the center of the universe and history."

The pope has also met and conferred with the heads of the religious orders. He has cooled off, temporarily at least, fiery dissident Archbishop Lefebvre, unrepentant founder of the Latin Mass movement.

The Holy Father also has to keep an eye on the Vatican Bank, and the pope's charities under Cor Unum for the relief of disaster victims and for development projects. The recent con-

His voice carries more and more authority as the voice of Christians everywhere. Billy Graham says, "When the pope speaks, the world listens."

Giulio Carlo Argan, art historian and independent, who was elected mayor of
Rome on the Communist ticket, is greeted by John Paul II to win fame as
"the Marxist who shook hands with three popes." Argan has since retired,
with much regret. He is internationally respected as a scholar and is the
author of the standard textbook on Italian art. He seemed the perfect choice
to rule a city filled with priceless mementos of the Caesars and the popes.

A family from Poland, their daughter wearing the traditional
Polish costume, delights John Paul and the crowd.

"I am a giver.
I touch forces that
expand the mind."

claves were a severe burden on the finances of the Church. Also taxing are the famine in Africa and the agony of wartorn Lebanon. Despite the vast art treasures of the Church, there is little cold cash in the Vatican strongbox. The last five popes died with almost no personal possessions. However, to quiet controversy, John Paul II has seen to it that a public disclosure of Vatican finances was made for the first time — revealing a staggering deficit of twenty million dollars a year.

In a history-making five days (November 5-9, 1979), John Paul revitalized the Sacred College of Cardinals, calling them to Rome for an unprecedented session. It was the first time in more than four centuries that the cardinals — though defined in Church law as advisers of the pope — were summoned as a group to discuss current Church issues with His Holiness.

In addition to finances, the cardinals were asked to share their views with the pope on the current structure and functioning of the Roman Curia and on the relationship of the Church to modern culture.

What will he do next? One thing for sure, he seems to outdistance his champions and his critics daily. He will outdate this book long before it even reaches the press. At this writing, he has received invitations to visit twenty countries over an eighteen-month period. Most probable trips? To Lourdes in 1981, during the International Eucharistic Congress, and a return to the U.S. in 1982.

He clearly does intend to rule the Church democratically, in collegiality with the cardinals and bishops. John Paul II will also continue to take the initiative ecumenically, embracing leaders of other religious groups. He respects the ideas and traditions of others. And he will discuss them at length in any of a half-dozen languages.

Everyone agrees that this pope is one of those rare characters who have a great capacity for hard work and yet have always found time for people. In Krakow his car was fitted with a special lamp and a makeshift desk so that he could work as he was driven along. In conferences, he often works on his own projects — while keeping up with all that goes on around him. He reads avidly, even on the run. Just before he was elected pope, he busied himself studying a volume on political theory.

This busy, dynamic man even sees himself as one who releases energy in others. In one of his poems he says, "I am a giver. I touch forces that expand the mind."

There is a new
surge in the life
of the Church . . .
stronger than the
symptoms of doubt,
collapse, and crisis.
— *John Paul II*

John Paul's devotion to Mary

Hail Mary!

One could say every pope is a Marian pope.

John XXIII left Rome only once in his pontificate, to visit Our Lady's Shrine at Loreto.

Paul VI wrote an apostolic exhortation on Marian devotion. And, on November 21, 1964, on the floor of Vatican Council II, he solemnly repeated the consecration of the world to the Immaculate Heart of Mary. When Paul VI closed the Council he gave orders to the Sistine Choir to sing hymns to Mary for a half hour before the final Mass. As concelebrants at that Mass, he personally designated the bishops of Our Lady's most famous shrines: Lourdes, Fatima, La Salette, and Guadalupe.

John Paul I chose "Mary, most holy, Queen of the Apostles" to be the "shining star" of his brief pontificate.

Today, however, John Paul II's devotion to Mary gets even more attention for a variety of reasons. Psychologists say it stems from the fact that he lost his mother at an early age and needs a mother substitute. Political analysts point to the Polish factor. His talk of Mary as the "Queen of Poland" is a political statement about where the true sovereignty of Poland lies. And it is a constant thorn in the oppressing hand of the Red rulers.

For many years, Wojtyla made it a practice to preach a sermon on the Feast of Our Lady, Queen of Poland, at Jasna Gora, the Shrine of the Black Madonna at Czestochowa. In May 1977, he stressed that Our Lady was queen of all Poles, and recalled the vow of King Jan Kazimierz in 1656. On the eve of the campaign against the invading Swedes, Kazimierz had pledged the whole nation to Mary and promised to work for social justice among the Polish people.

Even the man in the street recognizes the pope's devotion to Mary by the motto emblazoned on his coat of arms, "I am all thine, O Mary."

Add up all these factors, and a few more known only to the heart of His Holiness, and you have a most devoted son of Mary.

Witness his first trip as a pilgrim to the Shrine of Our Lady of Guadalupe in Mexico City. Next, he went to Poland to celebrate the 600th anniversary of the apparition of the Black Virgin of Czestochowa. Then he flew to Ireland to celebrate the 100th anniversary of the apparition at Knock of the Blessed Mother, St. Joseph, and St. John the Evangelist.

On his pilgrimages, the pope always addresses Our Lady as if she were present.

On March 2, 1979, the first Sunday of Lent, he recited the Rosary on Vatican Radio and announced that he would continue with the radio Rosary on every first Saturday in an attempt to revive this devotion.

In his audience of January 10, 1979, the Pope underlined the importance of the Rosary as a family devotion.

Pope John Paul has expressed the thought that the strengthening of the family is to be the principal aim of his pontificate with devotion to Our Lady (especially through the Rosary) as a principal means to this end.

The popes on the Rosary

The Rosary is my favorite prayer.

— *John Paul II*

This simple and profound prayer, the Rosary, teaches us to make Christ the principle and end, not only of Marian devotions, but of our entire life.

— *Paul VI*

The Rosary . . . is a form of union with God and has a most uplifting effect on the soul.

— *John XXIII*

Place your confidence in the Holy Rosary. Use this most powerful form of prayer with the utmost possible zeal, and let it become more and more esteemed.

— *Pius XII*

The Rosary . . . is also a powerful incentive and encouragement to the practice of Christian virtues, and these it develops and cultivates in our souls. Above all, it preserves and nourishes our Catholic faith.

— *Pius XI*

Prayer to the Virgin of Guadalupe

O Immaculate Virgin, Mother of the true God and Mother of the Church! You, who from this place reveal your clemency and your pity to all those who ask for your protection, hear the prayer that we address to you with filial trust, and present it to your Son, Jesus, our sole Redeemer.

Mother of mercy, teacher of hidden and silent sacrifice . . . to you, who come to meet us sinners, we dedicate on this day all our being and all our love. We also dedicate to you our life, our work, our joys, our infirmities, and our sorrows.

Grant peace, justice, and prosperity to our peoples; for we entrust to your care all that we have and all that we are, our Lady and Mother.

We wish to be entirely yours and to walk with you along the way of complete faithfulness to Jesus Christ in His Church: hold us always with your loving hand.

Virgin of Guadalupe, Mother of the Americas, we pray to you for all the bishops, that they may lead the faithful along paths of intense Christ life, of love and humble service of God and souls. Contemplate this immense harvest, and intercede with the Lord that he may instill a hunger for holiness in the whole People of God, and grant abundant vocations of priests and religious, strong in the faith and zealous dispensers of God's mysteries. Grant to our homes the grace of loving and respecting life in its beginnings with the same love with which you conceived in your womb the life of the Son of God. Blessed Virgin Mary, Mother of Fair Love, protect our families, so that they may always be united, and bless the upbringing of our children. Our hope, look upon us with compassion, teach us to go continually to Jesus and, if we fall, help us to rise again, to return to Him, by means of the confession of our faults and sins in the sacrament of penance, which gives peace to the soul. We beg you to grant us a great love for all the holy sacraments, which are, as it were, the signs that your Son left us on earth. Thus, Most Holy Mother, with the peace of God in our conscience, with our hearts free from evil and hatred, we will be able to bring to all true joy and true peace, which comes to us from your Son, our Lord Jesus Christ who, with the Father and the Holy Spirit, lives and reigns for ever and ever. Amen. — *John Paul II* (Mexico, January 1979)

The measure of love
is to love without
measure.
— *St. Francis de Sales*

Left: Greeting
well-wishers.

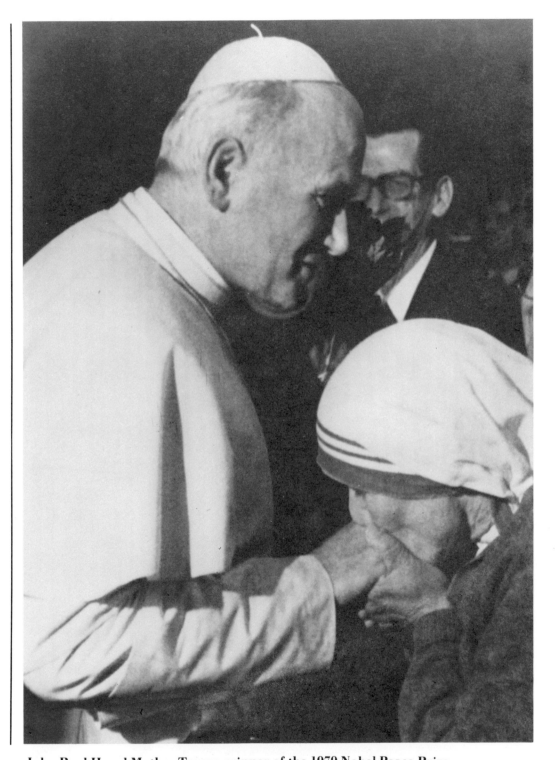

John Paul II and Mother Teresa, winner of the 1979 Nobel Peace Prize.

In Holy Communion we have Christ under the appearance of bread. In our work
we find Him under the appearance of flesh and blood. It is the same Christ.
"I was hungry. I was naked. I was sick, homeless. . . ." — *Mother Teresa of Calcutta*

I thank the Lord for
having given me
such brothers.
— *St. Francis of Assisi*

Great souls by instinct
to each other turn,
demand alliance, and
in friendship burn.
— *Joseph Addison*

**At a Polish audience, the pope embraces Cardinal Stefan Wyszynski,
primate of Poland.**

Pope John Paul II ordains his successor,
Monsignor Franciszek Macharski, as archbishop of Krakow.

The place
where men meet
to seek the highest
is holy ground.
— *Felix Adler*

All the beautiful
sentiments in the
world weigh less than
a single lovely action.
— *James Russell Lowe*

John Paul II meets with the then
archbishop of Canterbury, Donald Coggan.

Chatting with Mario Maltese and his bride after officiating at their wedding in the Vatican's Pauline Chapel.

The new pope signs a document during his first several weeks in office.

John Paul comforts a patient at a hospital in Rome.

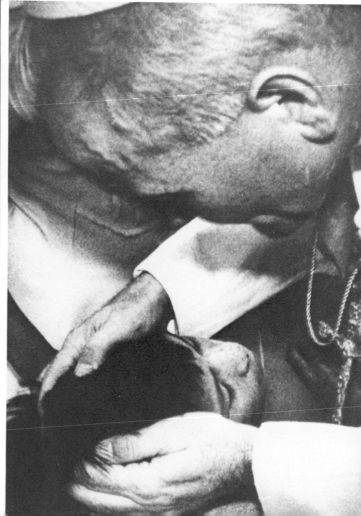

At a ceremony honoring Albert Einstein, attended by leading scientists, John Paul II calls for a reversal of the Church's condemnation of Galileo Galilei, who proved that the earth revolves around the sun.

As a face is beautiful because it unveils a soul, the world is beautiful because you see through it a God.
— *Immanuel Kant*

59

Here is my servant whom I uphold, . . . he shall bring forth
justice to the nations, not crying out, not shouting, not
making his voice heard in the street. A bruised reed he shall
not break, and a smoldering wick he shall not quench, until
he establishes justice on the earth. . . .
— *Isaiah 42:1-4*

In Assisi, home of St. Francis, patron saint of Italy, John Paul is greeted by enthusiastic Italians, and the sound of medieval trumpets!

Quotes . . .

The world esteems and respects the courage of ideas and the force of virtue.

We all know well that the areas of misery and hunger on our globe could have been made fertile in a short time, if the gigantic investments for armaments at the service of war and destruction had been changed into investments for food at the service of life.

Love builds, only love builds. Hatred destroys.

Human destiny is never worked out in isolation but in solidarity, in collaboration, in communion with others, through others, for others.

To be faithful is not to betray in the dark what was accepted in public.

The victory of the spirit must always have the first place in the scale of human values.

To bring about any spiritual renewal, it is necessary to begin with penance.

The Church is also a mother and spouse—biblical expressions which clearly reveal how deeply the mission of women is inscribed in the mystery of the Church.

Perhaps in these recent years there has been too much discussion about the priesthood and too little praying. Without prayer, this style becomes deformed.

66 Open wide the doors for Christ. To His saving power open the boundaries of states, economic and political systems, the vast fields of culture, civilization, and development. Do not be afraid. Christ knows 'what is in man.' He alone knows it. 99

— *John Paul II*

More quotes . . .

"

Prayer helps us to believe, to hope, and to love, even when our human weakness hinders us.

Are you perhaps still standing idle in the marketplace because no one has called you to work? The vineyard of Christian charity is short of workers. The Church is calling you to it.

My brothers and sisters. Do not be afraid to accept Christ and His authority....Open the frontiers of states, economic and political systems, wide realms of culture, civilization and development. Do not be afraid. Christ, and He alone, knows what is in men's hearts.

God takes delight in man because of Christ. No one may destroy man; no one may humiliate him; no one may hate him!

Beg of your Son, O Mary, such strength to the pope from the East as to enable him to crush all barriers and restore freedom to a tortured Church.

I worked in the boiler room of a factory for three years. I remember those years with great gratitude for the people, the good simple people who to me—an intellectual—were always kind and told me, "Sir, you've done your work. Now get some sleep. We'll look after things." And if it was necessary to stay over for the second or third shift, these kind people brought over their bread and milk and said, "You have to stay on, so have something so that you can endure it." These are small facts, but one doesn't forget such facts. During this time as a worker the deepest questions of my life became crystallized. (From "Homecoming for a Pope," by Tad Szulc, *New York Times*)

"

Once, early in his reign, the pope forgot to give the papal blessing. When reminded of his oversight, the embarrassed pope said, "I still have to learn how to behave like a pope," and gave the blessing.

Castel Gandolfo:
. . . the pope's Camp David

John Paul II is no "prisoner of the Vatican" like many of the popes before him. In addition to his constant pilgrimages, he has spent much time resting at the papal retreat at Castel Gandolfo, fifteen miles southeast of Rome.

In the first year of his reign he built a swimming pool on the papal grounds, to the delight of the Italian news photographers, the ever-present paparazzi, who can be counted on to violate his privacy.

Less enthusiastic were members of the conservative Curia who admonished the Holy Father about the expense. His reply? "It's cheaper than the cost of the conclave." Obviously, John Paul feels he has earned a few respites in his killing schedule.

You would find it hard to picture a healthier or more beautiful place than the Apostolic Palace at Castel Gandolfo, overlooking Lake Albano and surrounded by the loveliest gardens in all Italy. This is a dominating site, chosen as the papal summer house in 1623.

The shaded paths around cool fountains were part of the Roman Emperor Domitian's summer pleasure grounds. From the crest of a wooded hill, John Paul can look down the Appian Way's long, curved course toward Rome. At his side are tiered terraces, with a view of the sea some ten miles away.

From this hill, he can look with paternal dignity over the main street of the nearby hill town, flanked on the right by a scattering of café tables, and on the left by a domed church. On his own grounds, the pope has several villas, an astronomical observatory, a power plant, and a model farm that supplies the needs of the papal court.

The Apostolic Palace itself is an impressive structure that houses the papal apartments, reception rooms, and the living quarters for the staff. Inside, the long rooms are airy and spacious. Along the walls are a few paintings and several magnificent tapestries. The decor is most elegant and pleasantly restful.

On audience days, usually Wednesday when the pope is in residence, the town's streets are filled with up to twenty thousand pilgrims. They stream into a separate Audience Hall that has the same dimensions as the central nave of St. Peter's. To meet with the crowd, the pope drives down a road a short distance around a hairpin turn.

On Sundays the crowds pack the courtyard of the palace while the pope stands on a small balcony to recite the Angelus, a devotion the pope has strongly recommended be revived by Catholics everywhere.

When someone asked what he was doing at Castel Gandolfo, the pope replied: "I am working while resting, and resting while working."

Whenever and wherever John Paul appears, singing groups seem to spring up like mushrooms. Castel Gandolfo is no exception. The air is filled with voices of Austrian, German, Italian, and sometimes even a Polish choir.

In the autumn and winter the great palace's only inhabitants have been caretakers and a group of Jesuit astronomers. These days, however, the staff is always on the alert for a flying trip by His Holiness and his entourage.

Down in the village, awaiting the next trip of the pope, the villagers sit out the winter in their quiet houses.

These days their calm is being disturbed more and more often. After each of his historic pilgrimages, the pope has rushed to Castel Gandolfo for a few days of rest.

He is at home at Castel Gandolfo, more so than in Rome. His zucchetto slightly to one side, he walks laughingly through the crowd or sits (as his aides have seen him do occasionally) on a kitchen chair tilted against a wall, surrounded by people, exchanging wisdom and folksy humor with them.

Although his Italian is accented, John Paul speaks it well enough to crack jokes and understand other people's witticisms.

Castel Gandolfo has a long and proud history. From this place, Alban tribesmen went down to the Tiber River to found a settlement that became Rome. Heavy-sandaled Roman legions marched from barracks along this road to fight raiding Saracens and dug in here against Gothic hordes.

The old palace has been a stronghold, a retreat, a place of refuge in war. Today, it is still important as a source of rejuvenation for a busy, tired pope. It is, for John Paul II, a preferred retreat, a papal Camp David.

Left: Castel Gandolfo boasts a working farm and these beautiful formal gardens.

Right: Pope Paul VI arriving at Castel Gandolfo. It has been a favorite retreat of popes for centuries.

Crowds are
as enthusiastic at
Castel Gandolfo as
at Rome.

Below: Reception
room at Castel
Gandolfo.

"The pope is tired. May he get some rest?" John Paul asks the crowd for permission to retire. "Stay! Stay!" they shout back.

73

MEXICO:
. . . the "Miracle of the Mirrors"

**The pope arrives in Mexico City to
a tumultuous greeting.**

Mexico City

The stakes were high on Pope John Paul's first pilgrimage. In January of 1979, just fourteen weeks into his reign, he must have been sorely tempted to avoid going to Latin America, to open the bishops' meeting at Puebla, Mexico.

This third meeting of the Latin-American bishops was already keyed to the explosive issue of liberation theology — or social reform in the face of brutal dictatorships. Here is the Church's biggest problem area with three hundred million Roman Catholics living under varying degrees of oppression, in abysmal poverty. In the last decade, at least one thousand priests in Central and South America, enraged by conditions, have protested and paid for their interest in the persecuted by suffering interrogation, imprisonment, torture, and even death.

But Wojtyla, who remembers his own days in the Polish underground, could not resist such a challenge. He would go to Puebla, risk his reputation and the whole future of his reign.

"The pope is coming to save the Church. It's as simple as that," said one Mexican analyst.

Waiting for John Paul were the besieged bishops of Latin America and the people of Mexico, traditionally devoted to Mary, who could see in the Holy Father a kindred soul.

Despite a one-hundred-twenty-year attempt to secularize Mexico, the faith of the people has remained strong. Catholics still receive instruction in the faith.

Indeed, in the last twenty years,

I want to tell you with all my soul and strength . . . unemployment hurts me, conflict hurts me, ideologies of hatred and violence hurt me. . . .
— *John Paul II*

the number of dioceses has grown from thirty-four to more than seventy. There are ninety-four hundred priests, the majority of them Mexican.

> ". . . No longer will there be children without sufficient nutrition, without education. . . ."

Although these priests cannot wear distinctive religious garb in public, the government was prepared to overlook the fact that John Paul II would arrive in full papal dress and without a passport. (John Paul considers himself a citizen of the world.)

Ten minutes after he took off from Rome, John Paul II set a precedent by holding an informal hour-long question-and-answer session with reporters on the plane.

On arrival in the Dominican Republic, his first stop, this pope with a flair for symbolism knelt and kissed the ground. This was to become one of the trademarks of his pilgrimages. Where Columbus said the first Mass in the New World, and where he dedicated the Americas to Mary, the new pope now said a modern Mass before a crowd of three hundred thousand.

"Holy Father, there are millions of little mirrors down there, reflecting sunlight toward our plane. This is the way the Mexican people say good-bye to you...."

In a forceful sermon at the Plaza, John Paul called upon Christians to construct a "world more just, more human and livable," where "no longer will there be children without sufficient nutrition, without education. No longer will there be peasants without land to allow them to live with dignity. No longer will there be systems that permit the exploitation of man by man, or by state. No longer will there be families badly broken, disunited."

In that passionate concern for humanity the new pope actually set the tone for his entire pontificate. The crowd sensed this immediately, and gave the Vicar of Christ a thunderous ovation!

In Mexico the crowds were even more enthusiastic. After "Papa Wojtyla" the land would never be the same. Since the Mexican Revolution nothing has aroused the people like the presence of John Paul II. The spiritual response to his visit united the country in a spontaneous burst of national pride before the world.

A Mexican commentator said, "The history of Mexico can be divided in two: before and after Pope John Paul II. The people have shown the world the government can not replace the cross."

In just six days, the spiritual strength and charisma of one man effected a spiritual rebirth in a nation where civil authorities have been downgrading the Church for decades.

From the moment he arrived at Mexico City's International Airport, John Paul electrified crowds with his warmth and geniality.

The turnout defied counting. Millions greeted him at motorcades, Masses, and festivals. (Even hundreds of thousands of Americans crossed the border in their enthusiasm to see him.) His eighty-one-mile route from Mexico City to Puebla was lined by a wall of humanity. John Paul was greeted by confetti, fireworks, and floating balloons. Young people in Mexican costume — and even a few in Polish costume — danced for him. Their parents carried gifts: skis, a cross, flowers, leatherwork. They laughed when he donned a sombrero, applauded when he hummed a song to them.

The emotional high point of this trip came when John Paul rode to the shrine of the Virgin of Guadalupe, spiritual center of the nation. Police reported that five million Mexicans came out in the blazing sun to see the pope. Oceans of people cheered and waved yellow-and-white papal flags. During the Mass he frequently invoked the Virgin Mary, venerated so much in Poland and in Mexico.

Also noteworthy was the pontiff's

Above (right): Arriving in Mexico City.

Right: Mass is celebrated by the pope at the Independence Plaza in the Dominican Republic.

appeal to university youth. He is almost a cult figure with them, and their cheers verged on frenzy. Speaking extemporaneously in Spanish to students at La Florida College, the Holy Father urged his audience to study, learn, and work for the betterment of their nation. "Work for morality, for ethics, for justice. Work! Work! Work!" he pleaded.

As he turned to leave, the students shouted "Stay! Stay!" The warm strains of "La Golondrina" ("The Swallow") were played by the university orchestra. As the music and emotional cheering enveloped the scene, one TV commentator had to end his broadcast because he could no longer control his emotions.

The pope's presence in Puebla totally dominated the opening days of the conference, a meeting heralded as the most important of the decade, and twice postponed by the deaths of the two popes.

In his talk, John Paul II offered new directions for liberation theology, the most powerful and most controversial force in Latin America. "Jesus Christ," said the pope, "unequivocally rejects recourse to violence." (Politics *no*, justice *yes!*)

The pivotal issue in the pope's speech was one of tactics as well as belief. John Paul believes that more rights can be gained for the oppressed through moral education than by agitation and revolution. He rejects those who view Jesus Christ solely as a political Messiah.

Said he: "Whatever the miseries or

Regarding the pontiff's trip, one Mexican analyst said: "The pope is coming to save the Church. It's as simple as that."

sufferings that afflict man, it is not through violence, the interplay of power, and political sytems, but through the truth concerning man, that he journeys toward a better future."

When the time came to leave Mexico, His Holiness waved an emotional good-bye to all. Burly policemen rushed out of ranks to kneel and kiss his hands. Behind the throng of people, a huge floral display of white lilies spelled out: *"Gracias por su visita."* ("Thank you for your visit.")

Despite his weariness, the pope responded warmly to the huge crowds pressing forward to see him, to talk to him, to touch him. In all the trip, he never hurried away, or dismissed people in haste. Before taking off he held a press conference for over a thousand reporters. As could be expected, the papal flight from Mexico took off two hours behind schedule. An ocean of human beings, estimated at three million, crowded the papal route to the airport chanting, *"¡Viva el papa!"* ("Long live the pope!")

"He loves the poor, the workers and the *campesinos,* the sick and the children, and that is how he conquered Mexico!" is the way a reporter put it.

When John Paul's plane finally did take off, it circled above Mexico City for twenty minutes. The copilot said: "Holy Father, there are millions of little mirrors down there, reflecting sunlight toward our plane. This is the way the Mexican people say good-bye to you — with their Aztec sun."

The pope turned toward the window. His eyes welled with tears. From the air he blessed Mexico City. Far below, like sparks emanating from souls on fire, hundreds of thousands of Mexicans reflected back his blessing. At such a moment, who would dare deny that Pope John Paul II had indeed revivified the soul of the Mexican people!

John Paul II elevates the host during Mass in Mexico City at the Basilica of Our Lady of Guadalupe.

Hymn for John Paul II

Two thousand faithful slept in the streets of Guadalajara on January 30, 1979, waiting for the arrival of El Papa, the Pope of Peace.

Meanwhile, hundreds of children sang the following song ("Amigo," by Roberto Carlos, which has become Mexico's "Hymn to John Paul II"):

You are the brother of my soul,
really my friend,
On every road,
through every journey,
you are always with me.
Even though you are a man,
you still have the soul of a child,
which gives me friendship, respect, and
      tenderness.

I remember,
even though we have passed many hard
      moments together,
you have not changed,
no matter how hard the winds blew against you.

Your heart is a house of open doors,
you are stronger in hours of uncertainty.
In this difficult time in life,
when we look for someone to help us . . .
to help us find the way . . .
yours words of strength and faith
are proof you are always at my side.

You are my friend through all my journeys.
Your smile and embrace are witness to each of
      my arrivals.
You tell me truths with such open words,
it is not necessary for me to tell you all this;
but it is good to feel you are my great friend.
It is not necessary to tell you because you know.

    (Translated by Michelle O'Daniel;
    reprinted with permission from *Twin Circle*)

Above: At Cuilapam.

Above (right): Chatting with reporters on the papal plane.

Right: Speaking to students at the Basilica of Our Lady of Guadalupe.

82

POLAND:
. . . *a papal coup*

Triumph of Polish Catholicism

When a guest is in the house, God is in the home.
— *Polish proverb*

Almost immediately after his Mexican trip, John Paul II put his formidable political skills to the test in another country whose government was notoriously anticlerical — his native Poland.

As if to warn the pontiff against disturbing their domestic waters, the Polish authorities censored the pope's Christmas message to his Krakow diocese. They barred the pope from visiting the coal fields of Katowice and Piekary Slaskie where religious fervor borders on zealotry. They then postponed his trip from May of 1979 to June so that it would not coincide with the 900th anniversary of the martyrdom of St. Stanislaus, a hero of resistance to oppressors.

But they knew they were facing a losing battle. Poland is a land blazing with faith, the land that helped vanquish Islam at the gates of Vienna in 1683, a land that has foiled Marxist repression of religion for thirty years.

A thousand years ago, Mieszko I, first king of Poland, went on pilgrimage to Rome "to make a gift of Poland to the throne of St. Peter." Now, modern Poland had just offered one of its greatest sons to the Church.

Krakow, on the night the pope was elected, was a place of untold jubilation. In one university hall there was such a roar of joy, BBC reported, "the walls began to shake." Seminarians, students, and hundreds of thousands of the faithful battered on church doors to get them open. Once inside, people remained all night, deep in prayer. Other crowds raced to the bishop's palace to sing religious hymns and patriotic songs. The great sound of the deep-voiced bell on top of Wawel Cathedral, that sings only on historic occasions, was heard once more.

The events after John Paul's plane touched down at Warsaw are virtually indescribable. All Poland went a little mad!

Left: John Paul
greets his former
parishioners in the
streets of Krakow.

Right: At the
Warsaw airport: "I
have kissed the
ground of Poland
on which I grew
up."

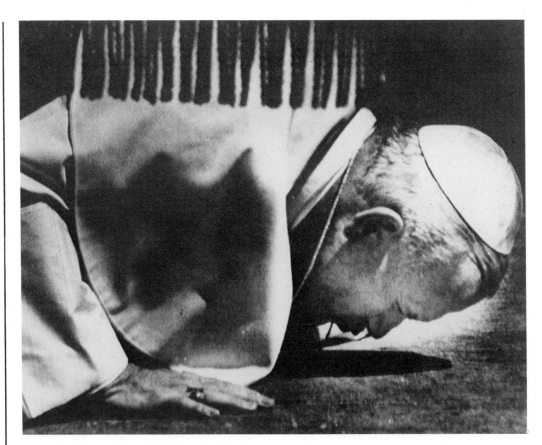

Despite official efforts to reduce the numbers of those who came to see the Holy Father, a sea of worshipers greeted John Paul wherever he went. The June air was filled with the peal of church bells, the sound of helicopters, bursts of applause, and the thunder of a mighty hymn: "Christus Vincit" ("Christ Conquers"). Raising his voice along with theirs was the first Polish pope in the history of the Catholic Church.

John Paul II, dressed in white, began his nine-day journey by kneeling to kiss the ground at Warsaw airport. "I have kissed the ground of Poland on which I grew up," he said, "the land to which I am coming today as a pilgrim."

Riding in an open car, the pope rolled through cities and towns en route to three dozen public appearances, all serving to celebrate the millennium of the baptism of Poland. Buildings and balconies were covered with flowers.

Streets ahead of the pope were lined with blossoms. Women in lace and aprons of traditional Polish costumes waved in greeting. Yellow-and-white papal banners fluttered in the breeze.

Despite a record heat wave, most of the people who came to see Wojtyla had to walk long distances on foot, and then had to stand for hours to the point of exhaustion. Their reward? To attend a Mass celebrated by a pope who was a native son, to hear the Holy Father praise their strong faith, to watch him hug their children, bless the pilgrims.

The pope's appearances were those of a virtuoso having a unique rendezvous with history, all characterized by an extraordinary joy — joy in the signs of national pride, in being human, in being a Christian.

There was no longer any hope of concealing emotions. John Paul could not hide his personal pleasure for a moment. He seemed exultant at the warmth of his reception. Unashamedly, he wept tears of joy. He broke off sermons time and again to start humming songs of his homeland. He spoke in the vernacular, and made good jokes and bad.

When he had to push his way through a crowd he kept repeating, "Please, please . . . the Church has to move forward."

When a small girl was placed on his lap to present him with a gift, she burst into tears, crying, "Mama, mama." "No, no," the pope said. "It's papa."

One night in Gniezno, where Polish Christendom's first see was established in 1000 A.D., after an open-air Mass for a hundred thousand young people, John Paul himself led his audience in a songfest. A record of his singing in Poland is now a worldwide hit.

When a group of young people began to sing the hymn, "Our God Reigns," the Holy Father spoke over their singing to say, "The last time I heard that hymn, I sang it with you!" As the voices of the young people swelled with the hymn, the Holy Father fought hard to remain composed.

All over the country, the people sang and waved and wept with him. They seemed to draw power from each other. In Czestochowa, a crowd of several hundred thousand sank to the earth as one, on their knees, at a single gesture of the pope, requesting prayer.

Carried away as he was, however, the pope was true to his promise not to let his emotions interfere with his mission. Every papal word and gesture challenged the rulers to allow religious freedom in Poland, and throughout the Soviet satellites, among the members of the "Silent Church, the Church Crucified." John Paul called himself, significantly, history's first Slavic pope, who now represented two hundred twenty million people of Eastern Europe. At Warsaw's Victory Square he said, "Without Christianity, it is impossible to understand the history of Poland."

A friend who heard him speak in Poland says he has become convinced "this pope fears no one but God alone."

At the shrine of the Black Madonna, in Czestochowa, where he spent three days, he stressed once again Poland's historic devotion to Mary, *Krolowska Polski,* the Queen of Poland. Legend has it that the Black Madonna was painted by St. Luke, and that Prince Wladyslaw of Opole was forced to leave it at Czestochowa when his horses refused to move from the spot. A shrine was erected there by the faithful. Later, the 1655 victory of a handful of Polish knights and a motley group of peasants over an overwhelming force of ten thousand highly trained and battle-tested Swedish troops was acclaimed a miracle, brought about when the Virgin and Child appeared in the heavens above the monastery.

There are many miracles and legends recounted about Czestochowa. In our own time, on August 15, 1956, on the Feast of the Assumption, one and a half million people converged on the shrine to petition the Virgin for the release of Cardinal Wyszynski, imprisoned by the Communist regime. They carried the primate's empty throne, in tearful procession, high above their heads, and on it put a giant bouquet of red and white roses, the national colors of Poland. Within a few weeks this remarkable and dramatic plea was answered — Cardinal Wyszynski was released.

Speaking at this holy shrine, John Paul said, "If we want to know how history is interpreted in the heart of the Poles we must come here . . . we must hear the echo of the life of the whole

Above (left): The Black Madonna of Czestochowa.

Above (right): A happy John Paul walks past the house of his birth in Wadowice.

Below: Speaking to a vast throng at Gniezno.

nation in the heart of its mother and queen."

At Wadowice, where he was born and grew up, John Paul had a rare private moment at the grave of his parents.

Only twenty-five miles away lay the town of Auschwitz and the concentration camp Birkenau, the worst hell-on-earth ever devised by man. There, the pope visited the cell of a beatified Franciscan priest, martyr Maximilian Kolbe, who offered his own life to save a fellow prisoner. His prayers and songs while being starved to death in a windowless underground bunker inspired the whole camp, and his influence on Wojtyla was profound.

By now, John Paul was tiring. When he faced fresh crowds who called to him *"Sto lat!"* ("Live a thousand years!"), his reply was: "If you wish me long years, then let me get some sleep." His voice was noticeably hoarse.

But there was still a mountain to be climbed, to the home of the *gorale,* the mountain people. Here, the Communists had built a worker's city of one hundred thousand, a grim, dirty town where God and His churches had no place. Gomulka vowed that never would any place for God be allowed within the city limits of Nowa Huta.

". . . This pope fears no one but God alone."

In his greatest victory before leaving Poland, Wojtyla had forced the regime to allow him to build a church for the workers on the outskirts of the town. He told a weeping crowd of fifty thousand: "This was built as a city without God. But the will of God and of the people who work here has prevailed. Let this be a lesson to all."

Now, on his return to Poland, John Paul set out by helicopter with Polish-American Cardinal John Krol (another *goral,* like the pontiff himself) to visit the church at Nowa Huta.

It was another emotional highlight for John Paul II as he held a Mass for workers while a crowd of a quarter of a million waved Polish and papal flags and shouted, "We want God! We want God!"

The Polish people, who had always known the depth of their faith, now saw it in a new dimension. Neither Poland nor the world would ever be the same again. The message of Jesus Christ was being reaffirmed again on the stage of the world theater.

John Paul II was himself overcome with emotion. Several times he had to back away from the microphone. Each time he returned, he found he could not continue. Finally, the crowd broke the silence by taking up the song "Boze Cos Polske" ("God Bless Poland").

The Poles will not soon forget this visit. Two and a half million of them crowded Krakow for the pope's final Mass to mark the martyrdom of St. Stanislaus. Cardinal Krol called the Mass "the most impressive manifestation of faith and devotion I have ever seen or hope to see." One reward: the pope has already announced that he intends to return to Poland in a few years. A hint that the authorities had better see that religious liberty is granted in full — or they will be hearing from him! Meanwhile, every week a Mass and homily in Polish is broadcast from Rome to Poland for those who are deprived of the opportunity to attend Mass in person.

A host of other papal trips are already in the planning stage. And John Paul promises to bring the same enthusiasm for social justice "through Christ" to each nation that he displayed in Mexico and Poland, and later in Ireland and the United States.

Clockwise (beginning at top right):

Cathedral at Gniezno, "the cradle of Polish Christianity."

Mass before the Black Madonna at Czestochowa.

Peasant woman at prayer.

A sermon theme: "Is it not right that this Slav pope should at this precise moment manifest the spiritual unity of Christian Europe?"

Above (left): Pope John Paul II kisses a schoolboy on the forehead during his visit to Czestochowa, Poland.

Left: Two million people jam Krakow for the final Mass of the pope's visit.

Right: A tired, happy John Paul sits beneath a huge replica of the Black Madonna.

John Paul II
in *IRELAND*
and the
UNITED STATES

Ireland, September 30

"Like Patrick," said John Paul II in Dublin, "I too have heard the call of the Irish."

He was the first pope in history to stand on Irish soil. One and a quarter million people, a third of Ireland's population, were gathered in Phoenix Park to greet *"Papa Eoin Pol II."*

He told them, "As I stand here, in the company of so many hundreds of thousands of Irish men and women, I am thinking of how many times across the centuries the Eucharist has been celebrated in this land."

In response, a one-thousand-voice choir sang the "Lourdes Magnificat," and Dublin's Police Band played everything from Beethoven's "Ode to Joy" to "Finnegan's Wake" and "Molly Malone."

Later, after a helicopter ride to the historic site of Drogheda, not far from the hill of Slane where St. Patrick lit the first Paschal fire in Ireland in defiance of a tribal king he later converted to Christianity, the pilgrim pope made an impassioned plea for an end to violence. The highway from Northern Ireland was backed up eight miles with autos, buses, trucks, and with groups carrying banners reading: BELFAST, DERRY, NEWRY, DOWN, and ANTRIM. Scarred and battered by ten years of horrifying violence and fifty years of discrimination and bigotry, these crowds had marched bravely past nervous, trigger-happy border guards to listen to His Holiness. He warned them, ". . . Do not believe in violence. Do not support violence." Again, "On my knees I beg you . . . turn away from the paths of violence and return to the paths of peace."

"I see the future of the Church,"

“ It is a day
of days,
a day of glory
in our lives. **”**
— *John Paul II*

said John Paul to nearly three hundred thousand young Irish men and women who gathered for a youth Mass at Galway racetrack. "Young people of Ireland, I love you," the pope said.

The response was overwhelming. The young people sang to him a most exotic range of song, "He's Got the Whole World in His Hands," the "Maori Love Song," "Waltzing Matilda," and dozens more.

Calling the Shrine of Our Lady of Knock "the goal of my journey," Pope John Paul II dedicated the Irish people to Mary in a Mass before four hundred thousand on September 30, beneath a fifty-eight-foot Celtic cross.

The Knock Shrine is Ireland's chief Marian shrine. In the hundred years since fifteen people first witnessed the apparition of Mary, St. Joseph, and St. John the Evangelist beside the tiny church in 1879, the site has become a chief place of pilgrimage.

On Monday, October 1, the Holy Father flew to St. Patrick's College, Maynooth, to meet seminarians, priests, and university students. Then on to the Limerick racecourse to celebrate Mass. The estimate that more than half of the entire population of Ireland saw the Holy Father in person during his whirlwind tour is not hard to believe.

World-famous flutist James Galway, a Protestant who studied with the virulently anti-Catholic Orange Order Bank in Belfast, performed for the Holy Father at the departure Mass at Shannon Airport. "This was the highest point of my career," he told a reporter from *Twin Circle*. "What an honor to play before a pope, and this one is a true man of peace."

Above (left): At the Limerick racecourse.

Left: Arrival of first pope in history to stand on Irish soil.

Right: Blessing the crowd at Knock, Ireland.

John Paul II in the U.S., October 1-7, 1979: "John Paul II is your friend!"

John Paul II's trip to the United States was easily the most exhilarating week in the history of the Catholic Church in America.

For the first time, a pope brought the message of Christ to a rich, indulgent, pluralistic nation where Catholics are in the minority. For the first time, a pope set foot in the White House. Just the logistics of his trip to Ireland and the U.S. are staggering. In ten days, John Paul visited twelve cities on two continents and traveled more than eleven thousand air miles.

His audiences ranged from a small group of U.N. delegates to the one million-plus who turned out for one papal Mass, while a worldwide audience watched his every move on TV.

Despite a grueling schedule of sixteen hours a day that left journalists limp with exhaustion ("The Holy Father isn't covered by the press, as much as he is pursued," wrote one reporter), John Paul still found time to go to a chapel alone each day and pray.

He seemed to gather strength, too, from the crowds hungry for leadership in a world where all is drab — the economy, the political situation, the energy crisis, the whole world outlook.

In seventy homilies, the Vicar of Christ met every moral, doctrinal, and disciplinary controversy head-on, stating clearly and forcefully the hard truths of the Church.

What a tribute it is that for one full week all America listened to this holy man and roared approval of his exhortations for spiritual reform. Seldom has one man commanded American crowds in such numbers, or moved them so visibly.

Catholics made spiritual retreats and found renewal in the sacraments. Young people held prayer vigils. Blacks, whites, and Hispanics joined together for peace and brotherhood. Leaders of all religious groups were amazed and thrilled. Somehow, the pope's pilgrimage struck an emotional chord, a hunger for faith normally masked from public view.

"He's telling us God is alive and well and calling you to radical discipleship," said *Worldview* magazine editor Richard Neuhaus, a Lutheran.

Evangelist Billy Graham called John Paul the new "moral leader of the world." Rabbi Marc Tannenbaum, national interreligious affairs director of the American Jewish Committee, summed up the pope's trip in one word, "Dynamite!"

Above: Mass in the pouring rain. But the huge crowd remained to the end.

Above (right): John Paul receives a tumultuous welcome on his first day in America.

Right: Old and young, rich and poor, believers and nonbelievers — they waited for hours, sometimes in a downpour. "The vibrations from him are just wonderful."

Boston, October 1-2

"I want to meet you and tell you all that God loves you, that He has given you a dignity as human beings that is beyond compare."

The start of John Paul's pilgrimage to the U.S. couldn't have been more dramatic. Imagine a pope arriving in the Irish Catholic city of Boston on the Aer Lingus flagship, the *St. Patrick*, from Shannon, Ireland.

Of course, it was a legal holiday. And the Italians from the North End were there too, at Logan Airport, with an eighty-piece band, to greet John Paul as his 747 touched down a few minutes before 3:00 p.m., Monday, right on schedule.

John Paul kissed the soggy tarmac and received a tumultuous welcome from Mayor Kevin H. White and First Lady Rosalynn Carter who told him,

"Americans of every faith have come to love you in a very special way."

First stop for the Vicar of Christ was the one-hundred-four-year-old Cathedral of the Holy Cross, where two thousand priests and nuns rocked the rafters with cheers. Then, the highlight of the day, Mass at Boston Common, where two hundred fifty thousand braved a bone-chilling rain to greet him. "America the beautiful," said His Holiness, "beautiful even when it rains!"

Most of John Paul's first major address in the U.S. was devoted to young people. He warned that "many people will try to escape their responsibilities: escape in selfishness; escape in sexual pleasure; escape in drugs; escape in violence, in indifference and cynical attitudes." Instead, he proposed "the option of love, which is the opposite of escape."

A weary, rain-soaked pontiff spent the night at the residence of Cardinal Humberto Medeiros in the suburb of Brighton. In the morning he changed planes, to the *Shepherd One,* and left for New York and a historic address to the United Nations.

New York, October 2-3

Every human being is endowed with a dignity that must never be lessened or destroyed.—*John Paul II*

The sun shone briefly as John Paul landed at New York on Tuesday morning. Here, he faced twenty-nine hours of activity that would tax all his strength. At the United Nations, where Paul VI had made an eloquent plea for peace in 1965, John Paul warned the representatives of one hundred fifty-two nations, once again, of the horror and foolishness of war. He also assailed the suppression of civil and religious rights, and the "frightful disparities" between the rich few and the destitute many. He also urged a pet project, the international supervision of Jerusalem, sacred to Judaism, Christianity, and Islam.

In Harlem, he burst into informal song for the first time on his visit, humming along with a spiritual. He spoke in Spanish in the South Bronx, urging Hispanic Catholics not to give in to despair. Then he wound up the day with a triumphal entrance into Yankee Stadium for a papal Mass.

The next day was one of the highlights of the trip. After a welcome at St. Patrick's Cathedral and a soggy ticker-tape parade down Broadway, the Holy Father delivered an inspiring address at Battery Park, with a mist-shrouded Statue of Liberty in the background. Then on to Madison Square Garden where twenty thousand young people staged a boisterous love-in. A one-hundred-piece band from St. Francis Prep in Brooklyn played themes from *Battlestar Galactica* and *Rocky*. And cheers reached a crescendo as the pope was presented with the symbols of today's youth culture — a pair of blue jeans, a T-shirt, and a guitar. John Paul was obviously delighted, and almost overwhelmed with shouts of "Polish power!" "Woo-hoo-woo," he cooed in the Polish equivalent of "Wow!"

In a farewell appearance at Shea Stadium, to an almost equally enthusiastic crowd of sixty thousand, the pope said: "A city needs a soul if it is to become a true home for human beings. You, the people, must give it this soul. And how do you do this? By loving each other!"

Right: A delightful moment at Madison Square Garden.

Below (right): New York went all out in a traditional ticker tape parade down Broadway.

Below: Addressing the United Nations.

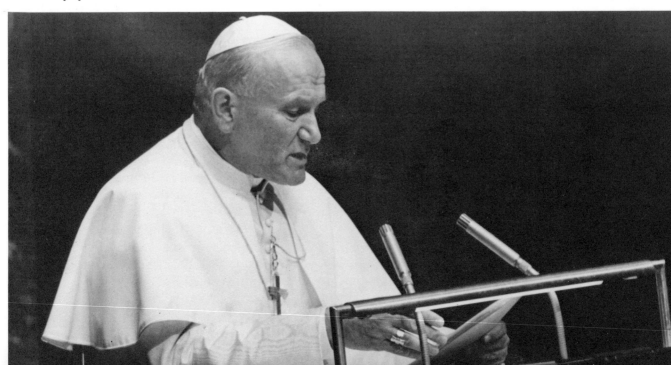

Philadelphia, October 3

The pontiff's red-and-white jet touched down in bright sunlight at Philadelphia Wednesday, October 3, escaping the relentless rain that had dogged his pilgrimage in Boston and New York.

On hand to greet him were seven hundred schoolchildren hoisting cards with the message, "Philadelphia Welcomes Pope John Paul II with Love." At a signal from Cardinal Krol, a good friend of the pope's, the youngsters flipped the cards over, spelling out the same greeting in Polish.

After greeting Governor Dick Thornburgh and Mayor Frank Rizzo, the pope rode in a bubble-topped limousine through heavily Italian South Philadelphia. One million people awaited him at Logan Circle for a pontifical Mass. Once more there was wild enthusiasm despite the fact that John Paul hammered once again on the hard truths of the Christian faith, warning especially against sexual "laxity."

The pope also visited St. Charles Seminary, the tomb of St. John Neumann, the Ukrainian Cathedral of the Immaculate Conception, and the Philadelphia Civic Center. In his talk there to priests and religious, he was equally firm: "Priesthood is forever. We do not return the gift once given. It cannot be that God who gave the impulse to say yes, now wishes to hear no." Another key statement: "The Church's decision to call men to the priesthood, and not to call women . . . expresses the conviction of the Church."

His words were strict but well received. John Paul asks of bishops and priests and laity no more than he himself gives to the service of God's people. Another part of his success apparently, his magic with audiences, is that he speaks with authority. He seems incapable of the perfunctory or cursory. He gives as much attention as he gets, which is most unusual in public men. And he loves his work. Not a hint of "splendid misery" comes from this cheerful shepherd of the world's largest religion. A Catholic deacon says: "The pope is the glue that holds the Church together. What better glue can we have?"

Right: Arriving aboard the *Shepherd One*.

Below (right): Pontifical Mass at Logan Circle.

Below: Philadelphia, the "city of brotherly love," says it in Polish!

Des Moines, October 4

On the Feast of St. Francis, and at the time of a harvest moon, John Paul II descended by helicopter in a rural setting outside Des Moines, Iowa, deep in America's heartland.

His arrival was a dramatic demonstration of a major emphasis of his pontificate — the importance of rural life, the rights of the rural poor, and the right to land.

Des Moines was selected because it is the headquarters of the National Catholic Rural Life Conference and of the Living History Farms.

This papal visit had a homespun quality different from the frenzy of the East. The pope stopped first at the tiny, whitewashed Church of St. Patrick's in the hamlet of Irish Settlement. At Living History Farms, an open-air rural museum, which recreates early farm life, the pope faced the biggest crowd in Iowa history — more than double the number that gathered for a glimpse of Nikita Khrushchev in 1959.

Because of the large crowds of people, police had to cordon off a sixteen-mile stretch of Interstate 80 and Interstate 35 for use as parking lots.

The Mass itself was filled with pageantry and song. At the Offertory, farm families carried symbolic gifts of soil, hand tools, and garden vegetables to the altar.

The pope, who had grown up in a predominantly agricultural Poland, told the worshipers, "Conserve the land well, so that your children's children and generations after them will inherit an even richer soil than that which was entrusted to you. . . . May the simplicity of your life-style and the closeness of your community be the fertile ground for a growing commitment to Jesus Christ."

To help that seed grow, Bishop Maurice Dingman of Des Moines is holding regional meetings of the laity as part of a year-long effort to capitalize on the papal visit.

Above: John Paul greets a child at Irish Settlement.

Above (right): With Bishop Maurice J. Dingman at Des Moines.

Below (right): A scene from yesterday at Living History Farms.

Chicago, October 4-6

More Poles live in Chicago than in any city except Warsaw, as the pope himself reminded his listeners. They responded to his visit with a huge outpouring of affection. And all their fellow Chicagoans joined in with gusto.

More than seven hundred fifty thousand people cheered John Paul as his motorcade roared along stretches of Nagle, Milwaukee, and Lawrence Avenues. There were Chicagoans on lampposts, trees, ladders, stairways, and roofs. There were signs in Polish, English, Spanish, and Italian. A computer-run billboard greeted him: "Coca-Cola welcomes Pope John Paul II to Chicago — 45 degrees — 8:20." At Cardinal John Cody's residence, John Paul rested while one priest reports that "they sent out for hamburgers."

Then thirty thousand people awaited him at Holy Name Cathedral, where the pope himself was treated to "Ave Maria," sung by opera star Luciani Pavorotti. Later, he himself crooned a soft "Alleluia" to crowds, then urged them, "Sleep . . . you must go to sleep."

On Friday morning, an even larger crowd waited outside the Providence of God Church in the Latino Pilsen community, where John Paul gave an address in English, and then in Spanish, to the delight of crowds who had

Right: A Polish banner, outside Holy Martyrs Church.

Below and far right: Mass at Grant Park.

Bruckner by what has been rated the world's finest orchestra, the Chicago Symphony, led by Sir George Solti.

If Chicago went all out in its admiration for this Polish pope, John Paul made it clear that it was a mutual friendship. "My stop here has been one of the highlights of my trip," he said. "I love the people of Chicago and I was very happy to meet them."

Mayor Jane Byrne, who had been first to receive Communion from the pope at Grant Park, added her tribute as the pope's plane took off for Washington, on its final leg: "Pope John Paul II, a pilgrim in our great city, has enriched our hearts, our minds, and our community in inestimable ways by his visit."

waited all night for him in thirty-degree temperatures. *"¡Viva el papa!"* they cried.

At Holy Martyrs Church, where the pope said morning Mass in Polish, two hundred thousand fervent Polish-Americans jammed the streets. Here, in his native tongue, the pope seemed more at ease, and frequently ad-libbed to the delight of the crowd.

Friday, all the Catholic church bells in Chicago tolled to announce the papal Mass at Grant Park. An estimated million people, shivering in the cool breeze from Lake Michigan, attended. The altar was banked by thousands of yellow and white mums, with the Chicago skyline as a background.

Among the enthusiastic crowd was John E. Wotylo and a half dozen other second and third cousins of His Holiness.

That night, at the cathedral, John Paul relaxed to a performance of

Washington, October 6-7

Washington rolled out its red carpet, literally, for Pope John Paul. He was met at Andrews Air Force Base, then greeted by Vice President Mondale, Secretary of State Vance, and Zbigniew Brzezinski, national security adviser, as well as by Cardinal William Baum and other Church dignitaries.

After fanfares from a band and a motorcade through the nation's capital, the pope celebrated Mass at St. Matthew's Cathedral to a joyous gathering of clerics.

Then, he became the first pope in history to set foot in the White House. Even the most cynical diplomats fought for tickets to the reception on the South Lawn. Both world leaders were given prolonged applause. President Carter hailed John Paul as "a pilgrim of peace . . . our new friend."

The 'Holy Father said he hoped their meeting would "serve the cause of world peace, international understanding, and the promotion of full respect for human rights everywhere."

There wasn't a dark cloud in the sky until the pope was challenged the next morning at a meeting with six thousand nuns. Sister Theresa Kane, speaking before the assembly, asked the pope to consider giving women full priestly rights. John Paul made no response. But when she knelt before him he gently touched her head.

John Paul gave his last pastoral message to the nation on Right-to-Life Sunday, as he celebrated a world-televised Mass before a crowd of one hundred fifty thousand. Worshipers shivered in blankets under threatening skies and a gale wind.

Holding tightly to the pages of his text, the solemn and fatigued pope stressed the sanctity of marriage, denounced contraception, and warned against the dangers that face people in a "society whose idols are pleasure, comfort, and independence."

In the strongest language of the week, John Paul urged his listeners to reflect on the "nature of marriage, on the family, and on the value of life."

Later, the pontiff told reporters, he hoped to return to America soon. "You Americans have supported me well."

This Sunday in Washington was no exception.

"We love you, we love you, we love you . . ." chanted the crowd. "I love you too . . ." the pontiff responded. He thanked the American people, saying, "Your hospitality has been warm and filled with love. God bless America! God bless America!" It was the pope's ninth speech of the day and the seventieth of a whirlwind nine-day, ninety-two-hundred-mile trip that began in Ireland.

Above: President Carter applauds John Paul II shortly after his arrival in Washington, D.C.

Above (right): Washington looked like Warsaw for a brief moment, as Polish banners danced in the breeze.

Far right: A tired photographer, a member of the press corps, is glad the whirlwind trip is over.

Right: Mass on the mall: "God bless America!"

A family scrapbook and brief biography

Karol Wojtyla was born in Wadowice, a small town fifty kilometers from Krakow, on May 18, 1920.

In that year, Wadowice was a place of ten thousand inhabitants, a center for the sale of wheat, potatoes, and beetroot, the local agricultural produce. A baroque church with its onion dome was a landmark then, and still survives. Wadowice was also a garrison town, and Karol's father (also Karol) retired there on a small pension from the army.

Photographs show a rather severe, balding man in a pince-nez, with a neat mustache, alongside his sailor-suited son. In examining his character, however, you find a cultured man, deeply religious, who won the deep love of his son, despite his strictness.

Karol's mother, Emilia, was a retired schoolteacher. Further details are yet to be filled in by biographers. We do know that Karol was educated in the public grammar and high schools of his native town with a heavy emphasis on the classics. And that despite attending a secular school, he managed to go to Mass daily.

Although the older brother, Edmund, was a physician of great promise, the Wojtylas found it difficult to make ends meet. Karol's mother sewed neighbors' clothes to make a small extra income. As mothers always have, she would amuse the people she

worked for with the prediction: "What a great man Lolus [a pet name for young Karol] will be some day!"

When Karol was nine years old, the first of a series of personal tragedies occurred. His mother died in childbirth. The baby girl was stillborn. Karol's only brother was forced to be away from home in a distant hospital during the years that followed.

As a result, from that time on, family life was limited. Hard work at school and sparse meals together with his father brought little joy to the exuberant youth. But there were some moments to be remembered. When on pilgrimage in Poland, the pope recalled with great feeling the time his father had placed a little book in his hand and pointed out to him the prayer to receive the gifts of the Holy Spirit.

Then, another unexpected tragedy struck. Edmund contracted scarlet fever while fighting an epidemic and died.

At this point, the young man was lucky to be befriended by a generous mentor, a priest named Father Zacher, who nurtured him through the difficult adolescent years. Lolek, as he was now called, became a brilliant student, active in every aspect of student life, including sports.

In 1938, when Karol and his father moved to Krakow, the cultural center of Poland, the young man came into his

Wojtyla dons an Italian alpine soldier's hat.

own. Krakow is renowned as "a gem among European cities." Without Krakow, it is said, there would be no Poland. By some miracle the city survived invasion, occupation, the worst wounds of war. While Warsaw was systematically devastated so that ninety-five percent of its buildings were in ruins by the end of World War II, Krakow escaped destruction. It still remains in some ways an echo of Vienna, with the flavor of the elegant café society of the Austro-Hungarian Empire to which it once belonged. Despite Communism, it still has eight full-time professional theaters, and many cabarets in which the art of

Above: Dressed for Holy Communion, in 1927.

Right: A family portrait in 1923, when Karol was two years old.

Above (left): Wojtyla (top row at left) with boys of local parish school.

Below (left): Ten-year-old Karol Wojtyla, second from right, and his father (man in center in overcoat).

satire, though circumscribed, is not altogether dead.

As a center of learning, Krakow was almost unique in medieval times. Its university, the Jagiellonian, was the leader in scholarship in the fields of science and philosophy, law, astronomy, mathematics, and geography.

Here, Lolek discovered in himself a real talent for the stage as a member of a student acting troupe, the "Rhapsodic Theatre." His strong baritone voice and his obvious poise helped him achieve early success. His friends were certain that one day Lolek would make the theater his career. Once, he did catch the eye of a visiting director who told him, "One day you will become a great actor."

Wojtyla is also remembered for being an exceptional student. One former schoolmate reports that he received the highest grades in history, literature, and languages. In addition, he was so good in Latin and Greek that his teachers felt uncomfortable.

Then, on September 1, 1939, the Nazi armies invaded Poland and the blitzkrieg brought the unready nation to its knees overnight. Karol Wojtyla witnessed misery, unspeakable cruelty, and death. No longer able to continue his studies, he was sent to work in a stone quarry. The appalling conditions the workers encountered drove him to the edge of despair.

His poem, "The Stone Quarry," reflects the pain and anger of those days, the knotted muscles, the cracked hands. Yet it also projects immense compassion, the sensitivity to human dignity, the awareness of love as a driving force of life.

Then personal tragedy struck again. His father died, leaving him alone, at twenty-one, in a savage world.

Karol was fortunate to survive. The only way to stay alive at that time was to have an *Arbeitskarte,* or work permit. Without one, he would be rounded up and deported to a slave labor camp — sure death. He did find work, fortunately, in a chemical company.

Meanwhile, his theatrical troupe continued clandestinely. The survivors of the original troupe, now an active part of the underground, performed in private apartments to invited audiences of twenty to thirty people.

Wojtyla's courage and bravery were beyond dispute. A friend, Jerzy Zubrzycki, told an interviewer from *Time* magazine: "He lived in daily danger of losing his life. He would move about the occupied cities taking Jewish families out of the ghettos, finding them new identities and hiding places. He saved many families."

Below: Wojtyla as a new priest.

Above: Which man is the future pope?

Right: Prayer at St. Mary's, a beloved landmark in Wadowice.

His interest in the priesthood may have been stirred in some paradoxical way by an almost fatal accident. His skull was fractured in a street accident and he was hospitalized near death. Semiconscious and in great pain, he meditated on the fragility of existence and felt an urge to become a priest and serve his fellowman. But he ignored the call.

Shortly afterward, he was again the victim of a freak accident. He was hit by an army lorry and knocked unconscious, narrowly escaping death. This second accident marked him for life. One of his shoulders is higher than the other, and he has a permanent stoop. But that accident, Wojtyla himself has confessed, resulted in his choosing the priesthood.

He became a good friend of Jan Tyranowski, a tailor, who had formed a lay spirituality group. Karol and five others studied the writings of St. John of the Cross, a master of the spiritual life who co-founded the Carmelite religious order.

Karol soon became seriously involved in his studies. And then, suddenly, he disappeared. Various fantastic explanations have been proposed to fill this gap. The truth is simple. The Faculty of Theology had been abolished along with the rest of the university and the three seminaries of Krakow. But Cardinal Adam Sapieha, archbishop of Krakow, had decided to welcome a few theological students into his episcopal palace. Once inside, Wojtyla and his companions could not escape from their hiding place, for they would have been arrested on sight.

On November 1, 1946, with Russian Communists now occupying his homeland, Karol Wojtyla was ordained a priest and said his first Mass at the altar of Wawel Cathedral. Few priests have had such an unusual apprenticeship! Now, however, his enormous talents were recognized, and he was sent to the Angelicum University in Rome. He spent two hard years there, often with no food, and was terribly homesick. But he was fortunate in several ways. He studied under the great French Dominican, Reginald Garrigou-Lagrange, and he also came to be under the wing of the substitute Secretary of State at the Vatican. At that time, he was Monsignor Giovanni Battista Montini, the future Pope Paul VI.

Wojtyla's doctrinal dissertation? "The Concept of Faith in the Writings of St. John of the Cross." His grade? The highest, *summa cum laude probati.*

While in Rome, Wojtyla gave spiritual and pastoral assistance to innumerable Polish soldiers and their families who had been scattered throughout Europe.

Upon his return from Rome, Karol was appointed curate in a small village, Niegowic, where he was much beloved. A year later, he was summoned to the prestigious parish of St. Florian's, in Krakow. His meteorlike rise had begun! Once again, the parishioners responded quickly to his humility, his austere life-style, and his dedication to the service of the poor.

One most remarkable clue to his character was revealed by his cleaning woman. She reports that he never seemed to sleep in his bed. She suspected that at night he would go into the church to meditate before the Holy Sacrament. Others have confirmed this.

In Krakow, Wojtyla became a good friend of the university students who still called him *Wojek* ("little uncle"). He loved to ski and canoe, and he often went hiking with groups. In 1951 he took a sabbatical to do studies at the Catholic University of Lublin. He went on to become a professor of moral philosophy at this school, and also taught moral theology in the Krakow seminary.

Corpus Christi procession in the cathedral at Warsaw.

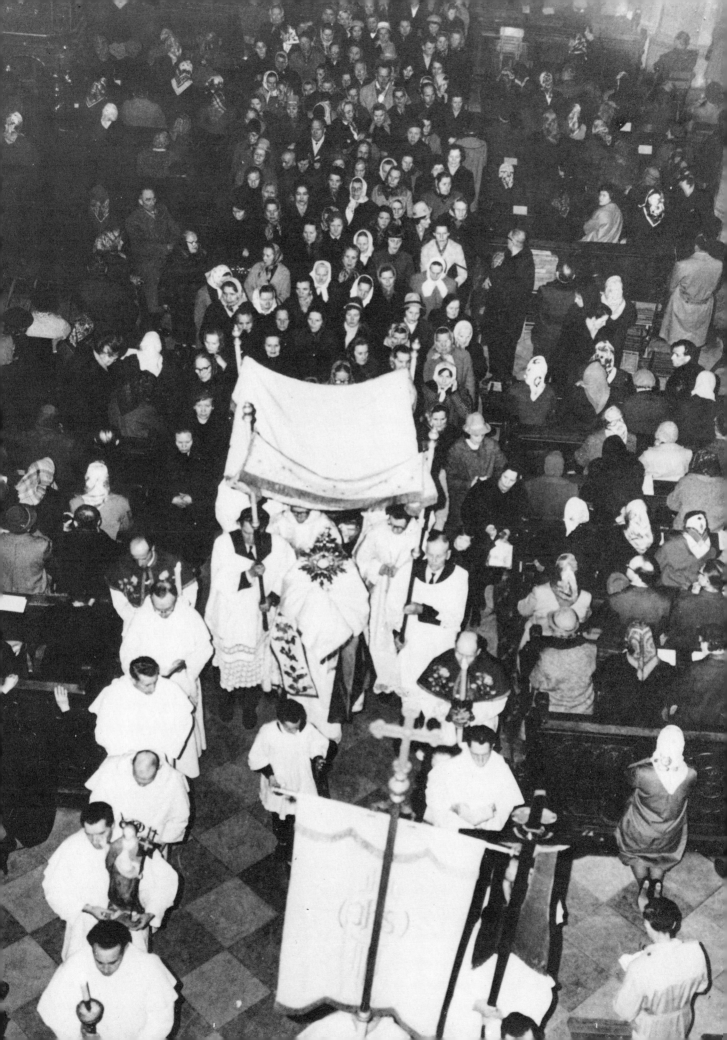

In 1958, Wojtyla was appointed an auxiliary bishop of Krakow. He was only thirty-eight, and on a canoeing trip, when he was informed of his appointment by his mentor, Cardinal Stefan Wyszynski.

The Wojtyla style was soon apparent.

Anyone could see this bishop: any morning, without appointment. They were all received on a first-come, first-served basis. The self-important would have to wait their turn, while some old person would prattle on about ailments. The atmosphere was much like that of a doctor's office. Wojtyla also held two-day seminars in the palace once a month for writers, workers, actors, students, priests, nuns ... who soon became his friends, and sometime companions on his outings.

His unique style must have pleased Montini, then Paul VI. He named Karol Wojtyla archbishop of Krakow in 1964. Three years later, on June 26, 1967, he named him a cardinal.

Wojtyla was still unchanged. He left his modest flat for the archepiscopal palace only when his exasperated staff forced him to do so by moving his few personal effects there.

The Second Vatican Council left its mark on Archbishop Wojtyla as much as he left his on it, broadening his perspectives beyond those of the Polish Church. He followed up on its decrees by establishing an archdiocesan synod and by educating his people about its teachings. His *Foundations of Renewal,* published in 1972, reflects those efforts. As a member of the Synod of Bishops and of the continuing Congregation for the Sacraments and Divine Worship, the Congregation for the Clergy, and the Congregation for Catholic Education, he returned to Rome, now a prominent figure, once or twice a year.

Pope Paul VI recognized his achievements by using him as a theological consultant and having him conduct his personal Lenten retreat for 1976, the meditations from which have been published as *Sign of Contradiction* (1979).

Cardinal Wojtyla traveled by way of Asia to the 1973 Eucharistic Congress in Sydney, Australia. In 1969 and 1976, he toured Canada, the United States, and Latin America. The latter visit centered on the Eucharistic Congress in Philadelphia where he delivered a moving homily on the human hunger for religious freedom.

In 1974, 1977, and 1978, Cardinal Wojtyla visited West Germany in a continuing effort to reconcile the Polish people with their former conquerors. These travels broadened his perspective on the world and did much to pave the way for his election as pope.

Back in Poland, there were moments of humor. Once, when Wojtyla went on a skiing holiday in Poland, a Czech soldier watched him cross the border into Czechoslovakia with interest. He stopped him, wondering who this distinguished person might be, sneaking into their land. When Wojtyla showed his identification card, as a cardinal, the officer thought it was a joke and threatened to cart him off to jail. "Nobody could possibly believe that a cardinal would go skiing," he said.

There was another case of mistaken identity in a holiday hostel at Zakopane. An elderly priest was staying in the room next to Wojtyla, and kept asking the younger man to fetch him cups of tea, take his letters to be mailed, and generally show respect for his years. Wojtyla did all the chores without giving the game away and later turned the whole affair into a joke.

Today, Karol Wojtyla has surprised us all by becoming the first Polish pope in history. And he has the whole world for his stage.

Cardinal Wojtyla impressed his hearers when he spoke at the Vatican Council on the Church in the modern world.

Let your spirit descend, and renew the face of the earth, the face of this land.

— John Paul II

If I had to sum up Karol Wojtyla in a word, his personality and his essence as a priest, I'd say that he is a man on his knees before the Blessed Sacrament. — Mieczyslaw Malinski (a friend of John Paul's)

It would take a seraph to say a Mass. If we really knew what a Mass is, we would die for it. — *Curé d'Ars*

No man desires anything so eagerly as God desires to bring men to the knowledge of Himself. God is ready but we are unready, God is near us, but we are far from Him. God is within, but we are without. God is friendly, but we are estranged. — Meister Eckhart (Dominican vicar)

Men esteem truth remote in the outskirts of the system, behind the farthest star, before Adam and after the last man. In eternity there is indeed something of the true and sublime. But all these times and places and occasions are now and here. God Himself culminates in the present moment and will never be more divine in the lapse of all the ages. — *Thoreau*

It is considered fitting that even the everyday language of the pope should be full of mystery and awe. But the example of Jesus is most closely followed in the most appealing simplicity. — John XXIII

The pope wants to be "the voice of those who have no voice . . . the champion of the oppressed."
— *John Paul II*

**Left:
Mass in the catacombs.**

The papacy is a martyrdom and a mystery.... — *Paul VI*

When the pope speaks, the world listens. — Billy Graham

No one ever came to me and said: "You will be pope." If only they had! I would have studied more and prepared myself. Instead, I am old and there is no more time. — *John Paul I*

You are he to whom the keys have been committed, and the sheep entrusted. There are indeed other doorkeepers of heaven, and other shepherds of flocks, but as you have received names in a manner different from the rest, so for you they bear a more glorious meaning. Other pastors each have their own several flocks entrusted to them; to you all the flocks have been entrusted, one flock under one shepherd. Do you ask for proof of that? It is God's word. — St. Bernard in Considerations: 2, 8 (Addressed to Pope Eugenius III)

The humble pope's most sacred duty is ... to live according to the teaching and grace of Christ so as to deserve the greatest honor of all, the imitation, as His Vicar, of Christ ... the Master, the only true teacher of all ages and peoples. — *Pope John XXIII*

Last word on the papacy . . .

**Bronze statue of the
Apostle Peter close
to the altar at St.
Peter's.**

66 . . . Man is God's image and cannot be reduced to a mere portion of nature or a nameless element in the human city. . . . [Each person] is a single being, unique and unrepeatable, somebody thought of and chosen from eternity, someone called and identified by his own name. . . . 99

Joannes Paulus pp II

Bibliography

Talks of John Paul II
Servant of Truth: Messages of John Paul II
(Daughters of St. Paul, 50 St. Paul's Ave., Boston, Mass. 02130)

The Year of Three Popes, by Peter Hebblethwaite
John Paul II in Mexico: His Collected Speeches
Return to Poland: The Collected Speeches of John Paul II
(William Collins, Inc., 2080 W. 117th St., Cleveland, Ohio 44111)

Pope John Paul II, by Mieczyslaw Malinski
Sign of Contradiction, by Karol Wojtyla
Fruitful and Responsible Love, by Karol Wojtyla
(The Seabury Press, 815 Second Ave., New York, N.Y. 10017)

Man from A Far Country: An Informal Portrait of Pope John Paul II, by
Mary Craig
(William Morrow & Co., 105 Madison Ave., New York, N.Y. 10016)

The People's Pope: The Story of Karol Wojtyla of Poland, by James
Oram
(Chronicle Books, 870 Market St., San Francisco, Calif. 94102)

Nights of Sorrow, Days of Joy — Papal Transition:
Paul VI, John Paul I, John Paul II
(NC News Service, 1312 Massachusetts Ave., N.W., Washington, D.C.
20005)

John Paul II, by George Blaznyski
(Dell Publishing Co., 245 East 47th St., New York, N.Y. 10017)

Illustrissimi, Letters from Pope John Paul I, by Albino Luciani
(Little, Brown & Co., 34 Beacon St., Boston, Mass. 02106)

A Religious Guide to Europe, by Daniel M. Madden
(Macmillan Publishing Co., 105 Madison Ave., New York, N.Y.
10016)

The author also acknowledges with thanks information on John Paul II reported in the following publications: *America; Twin Circle; Our Sunday Visitor; Sign; New York News; New York Times; Soul; Immaculata; Catholic Digest; Esquire; Chicago Catholic.*